Construct-a-Catapult

Developed by TERC
Lead author: Lee Pulis

This curriculum was developed by
TERC, Cambridge, Massachusetts.
Funded in part by a grant from the
National Science Foundation.

T E R C

National Science Teachers Association
1840 Wilson Boulevard
Arlington, VA 22201
http://www.nsta.org

NATIONAL SCIENCE TEACHERS ASSOCIATION

Shirley Watt Ireton, Director
Beth Daniels, Managing Editor
Erin Miller, Associate Editor
Jessica Green, Assistant Editor
Anne Early, Editorial Assistant

Art and Design
Kim Alberto, Director
NSTA Web
Tim Weber, Webmaster
Outreach
Michael Byrnes, Editor-at-Large
Periodicals Publishing
Shelley Carey, Director
Printing and Production
Catherine Lorrain, Director
Publications Operations
Erin Miller, Manager
sci*LINKS*
Tyson Brown, Manager

National Science Teachers Association
Gerald F. Wheeler, Executive Director
David Beacom, Publisher

NSTA Press, NSTA Journals, and the NSTA Web site deliver high-quality resources for science educators.

NSTA Press
1840 Wilson Boulevard
Arlington, VA 22201-3000
http://www.nsta.org/

Science by Design: Construct-a-Catapult
Library of Congress Catalog Card Number 00-131678
NSTA Stock Number: PB152X4
ISBN 0-87355-180-X
08 07 06   5 4 3

This book was prepared with the support of the National Science Foundation under Grant Nos. ESI-9252894 and ESI-9550540. However, any opinions, findings, conclusions, and/or recommendations herein are those of the authors and do not necessarily reflect the views of the National Science Foundation.

National Science Teachers Association

T E R C

The creation of these NSTA *Science by Design* materials builds on five years of research and development at TERC. This work was funded by two National Science Foundation grants: ESI-9252894 and ESI-9550540 and was directed by John Foster, David Crismond, William Barowy, and Jack Lochhead.

We are especially grateful for the vision, guidance, and prodding of our program officer, Gerhard Salinger, who was our GPS in uncharted territory.

We were helped in innumerable ways by an especially insightful advisory board: Joan Baron, Goery Delacote, Andy DiSessa, Woodie Flowers, John Foster, Mike Hacker, Colleen Hill, Gretchen Kalonji, Robert McCormick, Jim Minstrell, Jim Neujahr, and David Perkins.

The members of the TERC team who contributed to the development and testing of the Design Science units include:

Tim Barclay
William Barowy
Cathy Call
Judith Collison
David Crismond
Brian Drayton
Christine DiPietrantonio
Joni Falk
John Foster
June Foster
Riley Hart
Nathan Kimball

Felicia Lee
Jack Lochhead
Tasha Morris
Tracy Noble
Alison Paddock
Meghan Pfister
Lee Pulis
Jerry Touger
Margaret Vickers
Paul Wagoner
Kelly Wedding
Amy Weinberg

Special mention must be made of the enthusiasm, dedication, and long hours contributed by David Crismond and Earl Carlyon. The following hard-working consultants added greatly to our efforts: Hilton Abbott, Robert B. Angus, Carol Ascher, Warren R. Atkinson, Earl Carlyon, Michael Clarage, Jan Hawkins, Kathy Kittredge, Crispin Miller, James E. LaPorte, Kjell-Jan Rye, Rick Satchwell, Mike Stevens, and Ron Todd.

The authors of the final *Science by Design* units were William Barowy, Felicia Lee, Jack Lochhead, Alison Paddock, and Lee Pulis of TERC.

Science by Design: Construct-a-Catapult was produced by NSTA Press: Shirley Watt Ireton, director; Beth Daniels, managing editor; Erin Miller, associate editor; Jessica Green, assistant editor; Michelle Treistman, assistant editor; Anne Early, editorial assistant. Beth Daniels was project editor for the *Science by Design* series. The cover design and book design are by Camden Frost and Vicky Robinson of Graves Fowler Associates.

Field testing of the *Science by Design* series depended on the dedication of dozens of teachers and the helpful cooperation of their school systems:

Jerian Abel, Northwest Regional Education Laboratory

Bruce Andersen, Buker Middle School

Dave Armstrong, Lawrence Middle School

Henry Bachand, Mansfield High School

Hilda Bachrach, Dana Hall School

Ronald Bjorklund, Leicester High School

Marcella Boyd, Manchester Junior High School

Karen Bouffard, Governor Dummer Academy

Althea Brown, Medford High School

Lee Burgess, Lawrence Middle School

David Corbett, Whittier Regional Vocational Technical High School

Steve Cremer, Braintree High School

Deborah Crough, Long Beach High School

Ron Daddario, McCall Middle School

Raymond P. Gaynor, Reid Middle School

Elizabeth George, Westborough High School

Pam Glass, Talbot Middle School

Rick Harwood, Ware High School

Gary Herl, Tantasqua Regional Junior High School

Kate Hibbitt, Lincoln School

Patrick Keleher, Norwood Junior High School

Marty Kibby, Minetron Technology Education Office

Matias Kvaternik, Chelmsford Public Charter School

Jeff Leonard, F.A. Day Middle School

Walter Lewandowsler, Bartlett High School

David R. Littlewood, Agawam Junior High School

John Matthews, Southwick Tolland Regional High School

Eilen McCormack, South Jr. High Brockton

Scott McDonald, Needham High School

Brian McGee, Lexington Middle School

Bob Meltz, Manchester Junior-Senior High School

Charles O'Reilly, Lexington High School

Constance Patten, Lincoln-Sudbury High School

Fred Perrone, East Junior High School

Joe Pignatiello, Somerville High School

Doug Prime, Lancaster Middle School

Michael Rinaldi, Bedford High School

Thomas Rosa, Walsh Middle School

Eugene A. Santoro, Silver Lake Regional High School

John Schott, Smith Academy

Bruce Seiger, Wellesley High School

Douglas Somerville, Woodword Middle School

John Stamp, Manchester High School

Mike Stevens, Maynard High School

Michael Sylvia, Charles E. Brown Middle School

Syd Taylor, Mahar Regional School

Ted Vining, Monument Regional High School

Frank Viscardi, Framingham High School

This project would not have been possible without the help and critique of hundreds of students whom we regretfully cannot mention by name.

Appendix C: Sample Answers

Glossary

References

A NOTE FROM THE DEVELOPERS

Integrating Science and Technology

*C*onstruct-a-Catapult is aligned with the National Science Education Standards (NSES) in physical science, the International Technology Education Association (ITEA) standards, and the National Council of Teachers of Mathematics (NCTM) standards in statistics. Physical science concepts covered in this module include inquiry and design, dynamics, kinematics, and energy transfer. Through a variety of hands-on design activities, students engage in the iterative processes of scientific inquiry and technological design.

Compare these materials to a highway: if you rush straight through, your students will learn only a little about the territory they have crossed. We provide a number of interesting side roads that offer additional opportunities for investigating the linkage between inquiry and design. For your first trip, you may want to stay close to the highway, but as you gain experience, we hope you will drift further and further from the main path to explore other options.

Schedule and Cost

The time needed to complete the core activities is 13 class sessions, or about two-and-a-half weeks, with material costs totaling about $70 per class of 25 students:

- Design Brief and Quick-Build = $30 or less for a class of 25 working in pairs
- Research = $10 or less
- Development = $30 or less for a class of 25 working in teams of five
- Communication

KEY IDEAS

Elasticity

Hooke's Law states that the elastic property of matter is quantifiable for specific materials. Students measure force/stretch relationships of common rubber bands as the basis for a reasonably accurate projectile delivery system.

Energy

The conversion of elastic potential energy into kinetic energy is used to determine range.

Force

Force is studied and measured in the context of Hooke's Law and principles of gravity.

Calibration

Students calibrate and document procedures for their prototype in order to meet performance specifications.

Inquiry

The design process involves students in inquiry, generating solutions, development, testing, and evaluation.

Design

Readings on the history of ancient catapults (c. 400 B.C.E) give students a context for the background of a catapult's technological design.

ASSESSMENT

Student activity sheets may be used for formative or summative assessment. The *Snapshot of Understanding* is intended as a pre-learning index of prior knowledge. Students may compare their answers to those they give on the final *Snapshot* at the end of the last activity for a self-assessment of learning. Because group work is stressed throughout the unit, group assessment may prove more appropriate than individual scores. However, depending on your class objectives, homework assignments may provide the best measure of individual performance.

Portfolio Suggestions

Portfolios can be useful tools for maintaining individual accountability in a teamwork setting.

Potential Portfolio Items

The following student activity sheets can be accumulated in portfolios for summative assessment.

- Initial questions: *Design Brief*
- Individual information search: *Catapult Design History*
- Sketch of Quick-Build: *A Quick-Build Launcher*
- Brainstorming record: *Identifying Variables*
- List of variables: *Beyond the Quick-Build*
- Elasticity investigation design and results: *Investigating Elasticity*
- Group process description: *The Design Process*
- Part name labels: *Parts of a Catapult/Launcher*
- Fastener selections: *Resource List—Fasteners and Adhesives*
- Redesign reflections: *Beyond the Quick-Build—Second Pass*
- External feedback record: *Partner Team Feedback*
- Landing pattern analysis: *Making a Frequency Distribution*
- Force-distance graph: *Making a Launching Graph*
- Post-challenge reflection: *Reflections on Your Design*
- Prototype demonstration notes: *The Challenge Event*
- Group summary documentation: *Creating a User's Manual*
- Post-test and self-assessment: *Snapshot of Understanding*
- Oral presentation (Optional)

TASK	SOURCE
❑ *Students conduct independent information searches in context of human inventiveness*	AAAS 9–12, ITEA V, NCSS VIII
Standard/Benchmark: Issues in Technology; Technology and Society; Science, Technology, and Society	
❑ *Students build to specifications, manipulate, and observe interactions of parts in operation of a simple elastic mechanism*	AAAS 9–12, ITEA 9–12, NSES K–12
Standard/Benchmark: Systems; Technology and Society; Evidence, Models, and Explanation	
❑ *Students describe variation and identify variables and corresponding potential controls for improving design to meet performance specifications*	AAAS 9–12, ITEA 9–12, NSES K–12, NCTM 1
Standard/Benchmark: Systems; Nature of Technology; Evidence, Models, and Explanation; Problem Solving	
❑ *Students use elements of inquiry and investigate elasticity to inform design*	AAAS 9–12, ITEA 9–12, NSES 9–12
Standard/Benchmark: Design and Systems; Nature of Technology; Science as Inquiry	
❑ *Students use Newton's Second Law of Motion together with Hooke's Law to quantify component performance parameters*	AAAS 9–12, ITEA 9–12, NSES 9–12 & K–12
Standard/Benchmark: Motion; Nature of Technology; Technology and Society; Physical Science; Constancy, Change, and Measurement	
❑ *Students create tables and represent data in appropriate graphic format*	AAAS 9–12
Standard/Benchmark: Critical-Response Skills	
❑ *Students communicate, orally and in writing, their interpretation of this investigation and what variables to control in design development*	AAAS 9–12, ITEA 9–12
Standard/Benchmark: Scientific Inquiry; Nature of Technology	
❑ *Students apply abilities of iterative technological design, including brainstorming, research, ideation, choosing among alternative solutions, development, implementation, and evaluating consequences*	AAAS 9–12, ITEA 9–12 NSES 9–12 & K–12
Standard/Benchmark: Systems; Nature of Technology; Technology and Society; Science and Technology; Systems, Order, and Organization	
❑ *Students utilize tools and processes to construct and modify working models*	ITEA 9–12
Standard/Benchmark: Nature of Technology	
❑ *Students collect, represent, and statistically process test data to calibrate their design prototype*	ITEA 9–12, NCTM 10
Standard/Benchmark: Nature of Technology; Statistics	

TASK	SOURCE
❏ *Students create procedural operating instructions for others to use*	NCTM 2
Standard/Benchmark: Mathematics as Communication	

| ❏ *Students interpret and follow directions in the challenge demonstration event* | ITEA 9–12 |
| **Standard/Benchmark:** Nature of Technology | |

| ❏ *Students communicate quantitatively the technical performance specifications and operating instructions for their prototype* | AAAS 9–12, ITEA 9–12 |
| **Standard/Benchmark:** Communication Skills; Nature of Technology | |

| ❏ *Students articulate principles of science employed in a catapult's operation* | AAAS 9–12, NSES 9–12 |
| **Standard/Benchmark:** Critical-Response Skills; Science and Technology | |

| ❏ *Students self-assess their learning by comparing pre- and post-Snapshots of Understanding* | AAAS 9–12, NCSS VIII |
| **Standard/Benchmark:** Issues in Technology; Science, Technology, and Society | |

SOURCE KEY:

AAAS   American Association for the Advancement of Science. 1993. *Project 2061: Benchmarks for Science Literacy*. New York: Oxford University Press.

ITEA   International Technology Education Association. 1996. *Technology for All Americans: A Rationale and Structure for the Study of Technology.*

NCSS   Task Force on Social Studies Teacher Education Standards. 1997. *National Standards for Social Studies Teachers*. Washington, DC: National Council for the Social Studies.

NCTM   National Council for Teachers of Mathematics. 1991. *Professional Standards for Teaching Mathematics*. Reston, VA: NCTM.

NSES   National Research Council. 1996. *National Science Education Standards*. Washington DC: National Academy Press.

Go to: www.scilinks.org

Topic: force
Code: CAC01

Topic: energy
Code: CAC02

Topic: elasticity
Code: CAC03

Topic: mechanical
     advantage
Code: CAC04

Topic: gravity
Code: CAC05

Topic: mass
Code: CAC06

Topic: presenting data
Code: CAC07

Topic: scientific inquiry
Code: CAC08

Topic: friction
Code: CAC09

Science by Design: Construct-a-Catapult brings you *sci*LINKS, a new project that blends the two main delivery systems for curriculum—books and telecommunications—into a dynamic new educational tool for all children, their parents, and their teachers. This effort, called *sci*LINKS, links specific science content with instructionally rich Internet resources. *sci*LINKS represents an enormous opportunity to create new pathways to learners, new opportunities for professional growth among teachers, and new modes of engagement for parents.

In this *sci*LINKed text, you will find an icon near several of the concepts you are studying. Under it, you will find the *sci*LINKS URL (http://www.scilinks.org/) and a code. Go to the *sci*LINKS Web site, sign in, type the code from your text, and you will receive a list of URLs that are selected by science educators. Sites are chosen for accurate and age-appropriate content and good pedagogy. The underlying database changes constantly, eliminating dead or revised sites or simply replacing them with better selections. The ink may dry on the page, but the science it describes will always be fresh. *sci*LINKS also ensures that the online content teachers count on remains available for the life of this text. The *sci*LINKS search team regularly reviews the materials to which this text points—revising the URLs as needed or replacing Web pages that have disappeared with new pages. When you send your students to *sci*LINKS to use a code from this text, you can always count on good content being available.

The selection process involves four review stages:

1. First, a cadre of undergraduate science education majors searches the World Wide Web for interesting science resources. The undergraduates submit about 500 sites a week for consideration.

2. Next, packets of these Web pages are organized and sent to teacher-Webwatchers with expertise in given fields and grade levels. The teacher-Webwatchers can also submit Web pages that they have found on their own. The teachers pick the jewels from this selection and correlate them to the National Science Education Standards. These pages are submitted to the *sci*LINKS database.

3. Then scientists review these correlated sites for accuracy.

4. Finally, NSTA staff approve the Web pages and edit the information provided for accuracy and consistent style.

NATIONAL SCIENCE TEACHERS ASSOCIATION

Introduction
Read *Design Brief*
Take *Snapshot of Understanding*
Read *Catapult History*

Quick-Build
Make a Quick-Build catapult
Test catapult
Identify variables
Plan modifications beyond the Quick-Build

Research
Overview
Investigate elasticity
Collect data relating to *force* and *stretch*
Plot data
Analyze data
Summarize in formula

Development
Overview
Diagram and list parts of a catapult
Select fasteners and adhesives
Redesign catapult
Build catapult
Recalibrate force settings
Obtain feedback on revised design
Obtain distribution data of projectile firings
Plot distributions
Graph range vs. force settings
Reflect on design

Communication
Overview
Create User's Manual
Conduct the Challenge Event
Take *Snapshot of Understanding*

Design Brief

D A Y 1

The material property of elasticity employed in the catapult is used today by pole-vaulters. Since the inception of the flexible fiberglass pole, world records have increased by more than two meters.

CATAPULT DESIGN BRIEF

In this unit, you will be designing, building, and improving a mechanical launching system resembling an ancient catapult. Your system will be scaled down for use in the classroom and will take advantage of elastic properties of modern materials, saving you tasks like twisting huge bundles of sinew into torsion springs (see *Catapult Design History* reading, p. 13). You will use both technological design and scientific inquiry as processes to investigate and improve how your catapult performs.

Construct-a-Catapult Design Challenge

As a member of a product development team, you are to design, build, and document a mechanical launching system that can deliver a small object predictably and repeatedly over a specified range of distances.

Scope of Work

☼ Quick-Build: Build a design according to specifications.

☼ Research: **Investigate elasticity**, and identify variables you can control to create a more accurate catapult.

☼ Development: **Redesign**, build, and test; collect data and analyze patterns of results; then **calibrate** your prototype catapult with a launching guide and graph to meet the challenge.

☼ Communication: Produce a **User's Manual** that documents your design and its operation, including sketches, charts, launching graphs, and notes.

Key Questions: Write two questions that you have regarding your challenge and/or scope of work.

NATIONAL SCIENCE TEACHERS ASSOCIATION

What I Already Know About Catapults

SAFETY ALERT!

In this exercise, you will be launching elastic bands. You must wear safety glasses or goggles whenever elastics are launched and be careful to aim away from others.

The unit of study you are about to begin will challenge you to design, build, test, and calibrate a working model of a mechanical system most closely resembling an ancient catapult. Controlling the system will require you to investigate elasticity. Before you begin, record what you already know about catapults, forces, and energy by answering the questions below. This is not a test—it is a series of questions that ask about your current knowledge of the material in this unit. At the end of the unit you will answer very similar questions, after which, you can compare what you have learned with the answers you give here.

1. Using a rubber band as a catapult and a pie plate as a target, try to shoot a rubber band into the pie plate placed on the floor. Move the pie plate closer to you or farther away and keep trying to shoot the rubber band into it.

   (a) What important variables do you need to deal with as you try to hit the pie plate?

   (b) What scientific principle(s) can you use to describe how your elastic catapult operates?

2. What does a catapult look like? Make a sketch and label its parts or describe in words in the space below.

3. List any current uses of catapult-like devices of which you are aware. (For example, catapults are used to launch planes from aircraft carriers.)

4. Have you ever designed and built anything? (yes/no) If yes, describe how you went about your designing and building. If not, think about how you might go about designing and building something and describe below.

5. From your previous learning or experience, describe what the following terms mean:

force:

energy:

CATAPULT DESIGN HISTORY

Throughout history, humans have applied innovative ideas and designs to devices for throwing weapons. First, the sling was developed to overcome the limitations of the human arm. Next, hunters and soldiers devised the bow and arrow to improve aim and velocity. Eventually, major advances in power and accuracy were achieved with the design of machines called *catapults*. Early catapults were modeled after the bow and arrow, but quickly evolved into strong, single-armed machines constructed of composite layers of wood, sinew, and horn. This new weapon for attackers unbalanced the advantage once held by defenders during enemy siege (see *The Catapult Advantage* section below). While the defenders still had the ability to prepare for attack by building large walls, attackers—using catapults—could physically overcome these obstacles. These accurate machines also provided cover fire for troops attempting to breach enemy walls.

> Catapult *is derived from the Greek prefix* kata *denoting downward motion, and* pelte, *a light shield carried by Greek troops. A* katapelte *could literally smash a projectile downward completely through a shield.*

From Tension Bow to Torsion Spring

The first catapults were designed under the direction of Dionysius the Elder, ruler of the Greek colony of Syracuse, Sicily in 399 B.C.E. To prepare his city for a long war with Carthage, Dionysius assembled large research and development teams to create products that would give Syracuse strategic advantage in the upcoming war. The teams were made up of specialists who divided their labor into manageable units. Research and development enterprises still use this practice today.

Under Dionysius's direction, Greek artisans created the *gastrophetes*, or "belly bow," modeled after the bow and arrow. To cock the weapon, the archer pulled the stock—the compound beam forming the main axis of the weapon—into his abdomen and pulled back the string with both arms. Using two arms to cock the bow created substantially more power than the traditional hand-bow, for which the archer used only one hand. This tension bow was also larger than the hand-bow and consequently was able to hurl heavier arrows. However, the gastrophetes lacked the ability to throw arrows more than 300 yards and it was incapable of throwing stones.

To address the shortcomings of the gastrophetes, further research led to the development of a new type of bow: the *ballista* (Figure 1). This bow-like device was made of two independent lateral arms connected by a bowstring at the outer ends. Unlike earlier bows, the ballista used the power of torsion to propel stones. Bundles of cord or animal sinew were twisted to energize the bowstring; more twisting created a greater torsion effect and therefore more power. Although similar in form to the gastrophetes, the substitution of torsion for tension made the ballista a more powerful machine.

Figure 1: Ballista

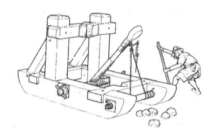

Figure 2: Onager

By the fourth century C.E., the latest projectile-launching device was the one-armed, torsion-driven, sling machine known as the *onager* (Figure 2) or "wild donkey," named for the bucking action it exhibited under the force of recoil. Unlike the bows used in earlier times, the onager combined both throwing and slinging motions, which extended the weapon's range. A single arm extended from the torsion bundle and ended in either a cup or a sling, which held the stone. The addition of a sling to the arm of this catapult increased its power by at least a third, and allowed the machine to hurl a missile in a high arc—over potential obstacles—toward a target. Today the onager is the weapon most people associate with the term *catapult*.

Falling Weight Devices

By the end of the sixth century, a new stone-projector called the *traction trebuchet* (Figure 3) had appeared in the Mediterranean. The traction trebuchet was a medieval catapult-like device that threw missiles with the force of up to 250 men. Nearly all catapults used at this time

Figure 3: Trebuchet

operated by a sudden release of energy; an exception was the medieval *counterweight trebuchet*. Similar in action to a seesaw or a slingshot, this trebuchet used the energy of a falling counterweight that was suspended from one end of a wooden arm. This propelled a missile that was placed in a sling at the other end of the arm. These machines were simpler to construct, operate, and maintain than those with sinew torsion bundles. Trebuchet were used throughout the Middle Ages and up through the siege of Gibraltar by the French and Spanish fleets in 1779–82.

Evolution of Catapult Design

Beginning with the ballista, early catapult engineers combined several design elements to simulate an archer's motions for consistent and accurate targeting. These included:

- *cams* to transfer rotating motion into sliding motion;
- *claw-and-triggers* to grasp and release the bowstring;
- *dovetail grooves* with *sliders* to form a moveable joint;
- *flat-link chains* to connect other design elements;
- *pedestals* to provide stability and support;
- *ratchets and pawls* or *winches* to allow incremental accumulation of applied human energy for increased power;
- *stocks* to form the main axis of the weapon;
- *torsion springs* to store the energy used to propel an object; and
- *universal joints* to allow rotation.

A number of design features that made their debut on catapults are still in use today; these include *sliding dovetail surfaces, universal joints, cams, flat-link chains,* and *torsion springs*. Examples of modern uses include:

- *cams* in racecars;
- *flat-link chains* in necklaces and conveyor belts;
- *sliding dovetail surfaces* in woodworking;
- *torsion springs* in garage doors;
- *universal joints* in automobiles and aircraft.

In addition to making significant advancements in military technology, catapult engineers used experimental procedures, derived optimization and scaling formulas, and performed advanced calculations that showed a

SCILINKS
THE WORLD'S A CLICK AWAY

Topic: elasticity
Go to: www.scilinks.org
Code: CAC03

Topic: mechanical advantage
Go to: www.scilinks.org
Code: CAC04

Torsion is the reactive torque (rotational force) that an elastic exerts by reason of being twisted on its own axis. Tightly twisting and then releasing two strands of rope yields rapid untwisting, demonstrating torsion.

level of engineering rationality not achieved again until the time of the Industrial Revolution of the nineteenth century.

The Catapult Advantage

Before the development of catapults, the strategic advantage in ancient warfare was held by a defending army, who fought behind walled cities. An attacking army armed with a catapult, however, was no longer at a disadvantage. The ability of the catapult to concentrate hits on a single spot rendered defensive wall battlements and armored siege towers vulnerable, changing forever the equilibrium of politics and society.

Even after the invention of cannons and mortars in the thirteenth century, catapults were still active on the battlefield because they were easy to construct on site and were able to do a great deal of damage with more reliable results than the inconsistent gunpowder of the day. They had the further advantage of positioning flexibility and relative noiselessness.

Today catapults can be seen in medieval re-enactments, engineering contests, and period films such as *Robin Hood*. Movies and television even use catapults to produce dramatic stunts—such as flying livestock in *Monty Python* and an airborne piano in an episode of *Northern Exposure*.

OVERVIEW—DESIGN BRIEF

Give students the *Catapult Design Brief* and the *Snapshot of Understanding*. Begin a class discussion highlighting the important design issues they should consider. For homework, students read about the history of catapults.

Construct-a-Catapult Challenge

Students read the following design challenge:

> As a member of a product development team, you are to design, build, and document a mechanical launching system that can deliver a small object repeatedly and predictably over a specified range of distances.

Advise students that they will use processes in technological design and scientific inquiry together to meet the design challenge. At the end of the unit, another team will operate their prototype in a final Challenge Event, using an operator's manual written by the prototype developers. For this reason, it is essential that the team write a User's Manual that effectively communicates the important elements of their team's experience with the catapult.

Snapshot of Understanding

Students begin by shooting several rubber bands into a pie tin, using an "insta-pult" developed in a fast-paced, 20 minute introductory activity. They then write short answers to questions about their prior knowledge of catapults, the design process, and underlying science concepts. The "insta-pult" adds a performance dimension to this assessment that will increase with student interest.

Catapult Design History

Students read for homework a brief, illustrated summary of catapult design in historical context.

TEACHING SUGGESTIONS

Hand out the *Catapult Design Brief* student activity sheets. Students will keep these and future sheets together and will bring them to class with other notes to serve as a record and reference for daily activity (and assessment) in the unit. Advise students that they will use processes of

MATERIALS

FOR EACH STUDENT
Student Activity Sheets
- Catapult Design Brief
- Snapshot of Understanding
- Catapult Design Hisory

Ring, Pocket, or Folio Binder
- *(student supplied) for keeping student activity sheets, notes, and drawings for reference and User's Manual*

Tools
- *safety glasses or goggles*
- *rubber bands*

PREPARATION

- *Photocopy Student Activity Sheets for distribution.*
- *Obtain "insta-build" materials: rubber bands and tin pie plates.*
- *Preview library and Internet resource information (URLs that were useful at the time of publication are listed at the end of this section).*
- *Devise rules of safety and conduct for the brief pre-test engagement activity (shooting rubber bands into a pie tin).*

technological design and scientific inquiry together and that other teams will critique their prototype with respect to the challenge criteria. Students must document their activity clearly and precisely in order to contribute effectively to the final team presentation and their individual portfolio assessment. Indicate which activities will be individually graded and which will be given a team score.

Snapshot of Understanding

Give students the *Snapshot of Understanding*, emphasizing that they will not be graded on this activity. Its purpose is diagnostic: to find out what they know initially about the unit's key science and technology learning objectives. At the end of *Construct-a-Catapult*, students will be able to compare these answers to answers to similar questions given at the end of the unit. Allow about 20 minutes for students to complete the *Snapshot*, then collect and retain.

Issuing the Catapult Challenge

Refer the class to the *Catapult Design Brief* and discuss the challenge statement. While it is important to spend some time discussing the challenge, it is important to move ahead rapidly and begin the introductory "insta-pult" activity.

Contextual Design History Reading

Assign the *Catapult Design History* reading for homework.

SIDE ROADS

You may, at some point, wish to extend student investigation of the history of catapults to include Internet searches. Guidance on conducting a *Structured Class Internet Information Search* is provided in Appendix A.

Quick-Build Catapult

OVERVIEW—QUICK-BUILD

Your first step is to build a simple model catapult for launching a projectile. You will be limited in time and materials to do this. The general design may be determined by your teacher, or by your creativity with the available materials. The idea is to build this experimental launcher as quickly as possible and try it out to get a sense for what is important in building your next catapult, which will be designed for accuracy.

Once you have put it together, take your Quick-Build to a designated testing area and try launching the projectile. Your goal is to find ways to predict and control where the projectile goes. Each team partner should do some launching and take a turn at observing, making notes, and retrieving projectiles.

Suggestions

- Put the pie tin target somewhere in the launching area and try hitting it repeatedly.

- Move the target to find a minimum and maximum distance (*range*) over which you can achieve some measure of control.

- Use books or boxes to elevate one end of the catapult.

- Experiment with different ways of hitting the target, such as low and direct vs. a high lob.

As you are building and testing, jot down notes so that you can refer to them later. Use your trial launch observations with the Quick-Build catapult to identify variables that must be controlled to meet the challenge of predictable and repeatable (accurate and reliable) performance.

- What did you see happening?
- What did you change?
- What happened as a function of the change(s)?

IDENTIFYING VARIABLES

Your catapult is a system of inter-related parts. You may have observed that making a change in the catapult itself or in the way you operate it can make a difference in the catapult's performance. Think of the variables you observed as belonging to one of two categories: *parts of the catapult system* or *user operating procedures*. In the table below, list these variables by category and describe the range of possible variation. Focus on detail and try to think of factors you can control or modify to improve the accuracy of your launcher. Use additional paper as necessary.

Parts of the Catapult System	
VARIABLE	RANGE OF VARIATION
Example: *Angle of the catapult*	*flat, between 0° and 45°, between 45° and 90°*

User Operating Procedures	
VARIABLE	RANGE OF VARIATION
Example: *How you position the rubber band*	*high on the nails, in the middle of the nails, low on the nails*

BEYOND THE QUICK-BUILD

From your list in the previous activity, select the variables that you feel contributed most (positively or negatively) to the performance of your Quick-Build. Suggest what modifications you could make to meet the challenge goals. Record your current thinking below:

Most Significant Variables	Suggested Modifications

OVERVIEW—QUICK-BUILD

In a single, fast-paced class session, students work in teams to construct a materials-constrained, Quick-Build catapult. Students use their Quick-Build to launch uniform projectiles (such as practice golf balls or clay balls) at a pie tin target. They record notes on the changes they make and on the performance achieved, and sketch a drawing with labeled parts. During homework and class discussion, they identify important variables.

Quick-Build

Students rapidly design and construct a crude catapult. They then practice firing a projectile at a target to determine factors important to accuracy. A team must be composed of at least three students in order to complete the testing phase successfully.

Identifying Variables

For individual homework, students reflect on their Quick-Build performance and brainstorm a list of system and operational variables observed, with ranges of variation. They contribute their list to a class compilation and discussion.

Moving Beyond the Quick-Build Launcher

After class discussion, student product development teams select those variables deemed most significant to the challenge performance goals, and outline design features to control them.

TEACHING SUGGESTIONS

Hand out student activity sheets and remind the students to keep all sheets together and bring them to the classroom with other notes to serve as a record and reference for daily activity (and assessment) in the unit. These will be critical to their successful development of the final team's User's Manual, as well as their individual portfolio.

Building, Testing, and Sketching the Quick-Build

This needs to be an active, fast-paced class. Allow students only one class session to build and test a Quick-Build launcher. Divide students to work ingroups of three or four—refer to these groups as "product development teams." You can leave the design wide open or suggest a very simple design such as that shown in the *Parts of a Catapult* activity sheet (page 41). If you want students to assemble by

MATERIALS

FOR EACH STUDENT
Student Activity Sheets
- Quick-Build Catapult
- Identifying Variables
- Beyond the Quick-Build

FOR EACH PAIR OR TEAM
Building Materials
- *scrap board or peg board*
- *2–4 screws, nails, or bolts, 2–5 cm long*
- *rubber bands of various lengths*
- *short pieces of string or twine*
- *projectiles*
- *pie tin target*

Tools
- *awl, punch, nail, or drill for fastener pilot hole*
- *screwdriver or hammer*
- *ruler (mm)*
- *pencil*
- *safety glasses or goggles*
- *recyclable 15–27 exposure flash camera*

PREPARATION

- *Tailor Quick-Build instructions and assembly drawing to materials obtained; copy and distribute.*

- *Select a uniform projectile and provide to all teams. Carefully weighed lumps of clay have the advantage that they will not bounce; but these require extensive preparation and maintenance. Other options include: practice golf balls, small bean bags, or pin cushions.*

- *Designate and arrange construction and launching areas for the Quick-Build.*

- *Organize materials for easy access.*

- *Determine student team sizes and formation strategies.*

- *Contact related workplace career representatives: science, engineering, history, avalanche control, military, etc. for establishing context and relevance.*

reading a dimensioned drawing, you may wish to dimension or otherwise modify the example *Sample Student Catapult Designs* to match your supplies.

Arrange the common tools, such as hammers and screwdrivers, so that students have easy access to them. Students who have rarely used a hammer or screwdriver may need a demonstration of safe and effective use. Intervention by you and by "student consultants" at critical junctures may also be required.

Each student should make a rough sketch of his/her group's Quick-Build and for homework fill in labels for all parts. If appropriate for your class, you might recommend that manual drafting, Computer Aided Design (CAD), or other technical illustration process be used for later inclusion in the User's Manual.

Homework: Identifying Variables

Set the stage for design improvement analysis with the *Identifying Variables* activity sheet. Students list all the variables they observe as they build and test their Quick-Builds, and specify for each the range of possible variation.

Students are asked to classify the variables in two categories: those that are part of the device itself and those more associated with the user. An example of each kind of variable is included on the student activity sheet. Some variables you might expect students to identify include:

Parts of the Catapult System
- kind of rubber band
- tightness of the rubber band
- angle at which the catapult is positioned
- stability of the catapult's base
- how far back the rubber band is pulled
- how far apart the nails are positioned

User Operating Controls
- how the user handles the projectile
- how the user positions the rubber band on the nails
- where the rubber band is held
- consistency of operator stance, steadiness, and concentration
- smoothness of release

Class Discussion of Variables

Compile a class list of the variables and ranges of variation students identified in their homework. You may want to make a large chart on the board and jot down students' ideas so that all students have access to the complete list. Use a class discussion to set the stage (and to level the playing field) for the next activity.

Planning Modifications

The product development teams should begin their work with the *Beyond the Quick-Build* activity sheet. (A team must be composed of at least three students: one to launch, another to mark landings, and a third to record test data.) Teams discuss and select those variables deemed most critical and controllable for success in meeting the challenge. They record, in words or sketches, their plans to modify or redesign a launcher to address the problems.

NATIONAL SCIENCE TEACHERS ASSOCIATION

Research

OVERVIEW—RESEARCH

You have assembled and fired a simple, inaccurate Quick-Build catapult. You probably observed inconsistency in performance (unpredictable landings) from your rubber band-powered launcher. To make successful improvements on this device, you will need to learn about sources of error (non-repeatable results) in both the mechanical system and in the human operating technique. You will focus first on basic research regarding elasticity, using your actual Quick-Build in the experimental set-up.

Scope of Work

✿ Work in pairs or teams.

✿ Research the science concepts relating Hooke's Law to the functioning of the Quick-Build catapult.

✿ Suspend known mass loads from your Quick-Build's rubber band(s).

✿ Tabulate and graph stretch as a function of applied mass.

✿ Use Newton's Second Law of Motion and the gravitational constant to derive force/stretch calibration values for the rubber band(s). This will tell you how far to pull the rubber band to achieve a certain range.

As you make design improvements to meet the Challenge conditions, you may need to come back to these basic research methods to test and calibrate new configurations of the elastic propulsion system. No matter how carefully you predict and plan, there may be mistakes or surprises; be alert and learn from them so that you can modify your experiments accordingly.

INVESTIGATING ELASTICITY

A key part of your catapult design is the elastic propulsion system. In the Quick-Build activity you experimented with common, convenient rubber bands. Did you notice any useful relationships between the force you applied, the amount of stretch of the rubber band, and the distance the projectile traveled? Did the projectile go farther if you pulled harder to stretch the band? Did you notice any limits or exceptions?

The following activity will help you discover and quantify the relationships between the elasticity of the rubber bands, the force applied to them, and the distance they traveled. Matter has some universal elastic properties, whether it be rubber bands, concrete or steel (skyscrapers, which are made of steel and concrete, sway back and forth several feet during high winds).

These properties were observed and described by Robert Hooke (1635–1703) in his "Hypothesis of Springiness." A contemporary of Newton, Hooke discovered what he believed to be a law of nature similar to Newton's Laws of Motion.

While Hooke's Law is an important discovery, it is different in scope and character from Newton's Laws. In the design of your catapult, you will look at ways Hooke's Law and Newton's Second Law of Motion are connected to each other and discuss the differences in their application.

Experimenting with Stretch

1. Select two rubber bands that are different in width, length, thickness, stiffness, etc. Name and label them, and record their dimensions and other distinguishing characteristics.

Band A: _____

_____

Band B: _____

_____

Topic: force
Go to: www.scilinks.org
Code: CAC01

Topic: elasticity
Go to: www.scilinks.org
Code: CAC03

Topic: gravity
Go to: www.scilinks.org
Code: CAC05

Topic: mass
Go to: www.scilinks.org
Code: CAC06

2. For each rubber band, attach both looped ends to projections as shown below so that units of applied mass ("weights") may be attached and hang freely. You may wish to secure your Quick-Build catapult vertically on the edge of a table or window ledge.

Horizontal view without weights:

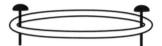 

Vertical view with weights hanging:

3. (a) Select a series of about 5–8 known masses to suspend from each rubber band. Your least mass must be sufficient to produce measurable stretch.

   (b) Tape a paper strip to your Quick-Build board and mark the vertical location of the unweighted rubber band as the starting point for your measurements.

   (c) Using paper clips or other hooks, attach each mass in sequence from least to greatest to the suspended rubber band, and measure the amount of stretch.

4. For each rubber band, record the applied masses in kilograms and corresponding distance stretched in a table of data points. Plot your data as graphs similar to those shown below. For each graph draw the best-fit line through the points. Tape each rubber band to the legend of its graph.

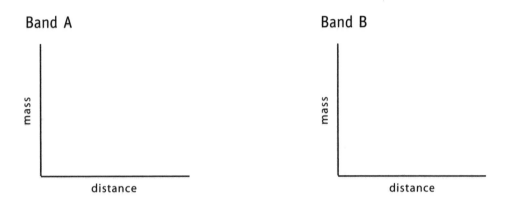

Band A

mass

distance

Band B

mass

distance

5. (a) Describe what you noticed about the points plotted for each rubber band.

(b) Could a straight line include all or most of your data for each rubber band? Explain.

6. Use your graph to predict the distance of stretch for masses smaller and larger than those you used.
   (a) How accurate do you think these predictions will be? Explain.

(b) Pick a mass between that of two you used. For example, if you had used 45 grams and 60 grams in your calibration, choose a mass in between—perhaps 55 grams. Figure out the length of the stretch corresponding to this applied mass.

(c) What do you think happens in the case of very large applied masses? Explain.

7. Try to express the relationship between mass and distance as a formula.

8. Hooke's Law states that the stretch is proportional to the mass you applied. The region in which a material—in this case the rubber band—obeys Hooke's Law is called the *elastic limit* of the material.

(a) What does your graph tell you about the elasticity of your rubber bands?

(b) How are your bands' elastic limits represented on your graph? Can you find a region on the graph where Hooke's Law is not followed?

NATIONAL SCIENCE TEACHERS ASSOCIATION

9. (a) Plot both lines from the graphs you made in question 4 on the same set of coordinates.

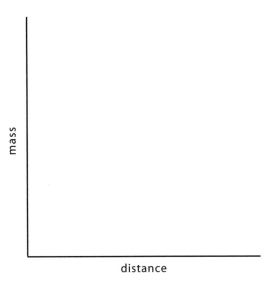

(b) Compare the two lines and explain similarities and differences between them. Be sure to compare them with regard to their conformity to expectations from Hooke's Law.

(c) What do you think the area under your plotted lines represents?

10. How could this exercise help you design your mechanical launching system?

MATERIALS

FOR EACH STUDENT
Activity Sheets
- Overview—Research
- Investigating Elasticity
- Projectile Motion
  (optional)

FOR EACH TEAM
- *clamps or duct tape for stabilizing each Quick-Build in vertical position for mass loading*
- *four to six types of rubber bands, about 25 of each type (ways in which they can differ include their width, length, thickness, and stiffness)*
- *set of masses*
- *graph paper*
- *paper clips or hooks for suspending masses*

FOR CLASS
- *accurate scale or balance for quantifying mass load values in grams*

PREPARATION

- *Devise ways of affixing Quick-Builds on edge vertically for the experimental set-ups.*
- *Determine suitable type, quantity, and variety of mass loads for appropriate stretch of rubber bands.*

OVERVIEW—RESEARCH

Students work in pairs or teams to investigate elasticity. They suspend known mass loads from rubber bands in an experimental design that uses their Quick-Build launchers. Students then create a data table and a graph to show the amount of stretch as a function of applied mass. They use the gravitational constant and Newton's Second Law of Motion to convert the mass loads applied to the rubber bands on their catapults into force calibration values; they also relate their data to Hooke's Law. In calibrating the rubber band, students are creating a measurement scale that relates the amount of stretch to the quantity of force (and hence the range the projectile will travel). As an option, you may consider graphic and/or mathematical derivations of spring constants and energy factors.

Time Requirement

This unit requires three class sessions:
- One class for experimental set-up, mass loading, and stretch measurement for two different rubber bands. You might assign the graphing of data for homework.

- One class for whole-group comparison of graphs and merging separate graphs to a single set of axes.

- One class for discussion of concepts, formulas, and steps for conversion from suspended mass to spring force loading in context of Hooke's Law, applied to a Quick-Build catapult propulsion system.

TEACHING SUGGESTIONS
DAY 1

Ask students to work in pairs on the *Investigating Elasticity* student activity. Attach the Quick-Build launchers to a vertical surface so they can be used as elastic supports.

Students will suspend masses in increasing increments from rubber bands and create a data table of mass vs. stretch for two different rubber bands. Comparing findings across the class should lead to appreciation of the numerous variables inherent in the elastic component of the propulsion subsystem.

Using the Quick-Build in the experimental set-up makes the data directly relevant to subsequent redesign activity. Students should complete data collection and organize their results in a table during this class session. They will then construct a graph for each set of data in the table and answer the series of homework questions in the activity sheet.

DAY 2

Review homework by choosing several groups of students to sketch or project their graphs on the board for use as a basis of discussion. Ask them to display the rubber bands associated with each graph. In order to assess the level of class understanding, pose questions and elicit responses from a range of students. Sample questions might include:

- What do these graphs tell us about the elastic behavior of the rubber bands?
- Why are the graphs different? [Relate to observed properties of each elastic band, such as length, width, thickness, stiffness, etc.].
- How are the bands' elastic limits represented on these graphs?

A straight line will describe the data within each band's limits of elasticity. The students' own findings should set the stage for your presentation of the formula for Hooke's Law and discussion of elastic limits. A change in line slope, or the beginning of curvature, indicates the deformation zone, where stretch is partially irreversible.

Hooke's Law states that force is proportional to stretch and is expressed by the formula: $F = kd$

This is sometimes written as $F = -kd$ to show that the force is in the opposite direction as the stretch. Students are often confused by the fact that this formula is sometimes written with a minus sign and sometimes not. The minus sign is important when we are concerned with the direction of the force. When the stretch is no longer proportional to force (when twice the force produces less than twice the stretch) you have exceeded the elastic limit of the rubber band. You have also permanently changed its properties.

Correlations between Newton's Second Law and Hooke's Law will be explored in the second day of this activity. On the first day, students should process their observations somewhat subjectively, gaining experience in how to select an elastic band for their next launcher's propulsion system that will remain within elastic limits. Students should come to understand that if they load their catapult's rubber band beyond its elastic limit, the permanent deformation will change subsequent performance, and hence render calibrations useless. For the remainder of the session, guide student groups in choosing an appropriate scale such that their graphs fit onto one set of axes. Students should complete the *Investigating Elasticity* activity sheet in class.

Answers to questions 9 and 10 should reflect the outcomes of the previous in-class discussion. Ask several groups to report how their observations agree or differ with their expectations and assumptions. Discuss any lingering misconceptions, and summarize conclusions.

DAY 3

In this session, students integrate the idea of force into their design considerations regarding elastic stretch. One way to make this transition is to use the following line of questioning (begin the class with a discussion about what causes the stretch in the rubber bands they have been using):

- *What causes the stretch and how does it happen?*
  [Force attributable to the pull of gravity]

- *Can you think of a place where using applied mass would produce less stretch?*
  [The moon, because its gravitational force is weaker (about 1/6 that of the Earth)]

- *Can you think of a place where there would be no stretch at all?*
  [In orbit, where there is no effective gravitational pull]

Next write the equation F = ma on the board to illustrate Newton's Second Law of Motion. Ask students to consider how the masses (in kilograms) that they suspended can be equated to forces (in Newtons). See if they remember that the acceleration of gravity is 9.8 meters per second squared (m/s^2), and know how this information can be used to calculate the force applied by a hanging mass.

On the chart they made earlier, students recorded the number of units of applied mass and the corresponding distances the elastic stretched in each case. By multiplying each total applied mass (in kilograms) by 9.8 m/s^2, they can obtain the applied force (in Newtons) for each case.

Have students describe what they have done in their own words to assess whether they understand that they have quantified the force that a specified amount of hanging mass exerts (vertically) on their elastics. Do they further understand that their graphs now allow them to quantitatively describe the force they apply by hand, when the catapult is in operating position? Just by measuring *stretch* they have force-calibrated the catapult. It is important for students to understand that it is the *stretch* in the rubber band that determines force, not the length of the band, which will not be zero when the force is zero. Furthermore, the rubber band need not be part of the catapult. If the catapult were cocked with a lever, a rubber band pulling on that lever could still be used to calibrate the force exerted at different angles of the lever.

As a further demonstration, you may wish to hook a spring scale calibrated in Newtons onto a rubber band and pull it by hand for verification of the calibration.

To expand class involvement with science and math, you may wish to develop the concept that the area under each line in their graph represents the energy applied and stored. You might also wish to develop a

classification of rubber bands by spring constants (k). Students can use Hooke's Law ($F = kd$), to calculate k. This can be done algebraically from their data tables, or by simply measuring slopes from their graphs. Students can discuss what higher and lower values for spring constants imply with respect to catapult performance.

The optional *Projectile Motion* student activity sheet (located in Appendix A, page 76) addresses air friction as one of the factors in calculating projectile velocity. Other factors you and your students may wish to consider are: humidity, temperature, projectile spin, density of the air at different altitudes, surface roughness and shape, velocity of the projectile, and aerodynamic lift.

SIDE ROADS

Independent Science and Math Investigations

You may be interested in having your students conduct additional independent investigations of elastics as further extensions of science and math applications. Some of the questions you may ask them to pursue are the following:

- Compare the effect of using more than one rubber band (in parallel or series) vs. using just one. Graph your results.

- Choose five different rubber bands and rank them from strongest to weakest. Graph your results.

- Choose five different rubber bands and rank them from most to least stretchy. Graph your results.

- Try some different configurations with your rubber bands (such as twisted, supported at greater or less initial tension, etc.) and compare the data you collect with that collected during class.

- Develop an explanation for what the area under the lines represents in your graph from the *Investigating Elasticity* homework assignment. Identify the relevant field of mathematics for quantifying the physical entity.

Development

OVERVIEW—DEVELOPMENT

You have completed basic experiments investigating elasticity. You have also reflected on the variables you need to control for improved catapult system and operator performance. To meet the *Construct-a-Catapult* Design Challenge, you will use your research findings to develop a prototype and create a calibrated, predictable firing guide for others to use. You will need to test fire (and modify if necessary) your prototype until a consistent pattern—and statistical relationship—can be found between projectile landing distance and force applied. You are encouraged to expose your prototype to the scrutiny of other teams to supplement your internal evaluation and revision cycle.

Scope of Work

☼ Track and record milestones of your team's work in terms of the design process cycle.

☼ Build your prototype and test its performance.

☼ Measure and record projectile landing patterns correlating to forces applied.

☼ Modify design as necessary until your data are consistent enough for you to develop written instructions for a new user operating your catapult prototype.

☼ Exchange your prototype and operating instructions with another team to obtain peer feedback.

Evaluate your prototype critically and make modifications until you are satisfied with its improved performance, or are simply out of time. Remember to reflect on your process; how you go about your design and what you learn are key elements in the communication and assessment activities to follow. Good planning is essential to good design. Look again at the results of your research where you identified variables and wrote about the key differences in requirements for catapult performance. Brainstorm with your team to maximize identification of improvement alternatives—be creative. Review *Inquiry Process* and *Design Process* resource sheets (available from your teacher) and be aware of where you are and where you are going in these iterative process cycles.

PARTS OF A CATAPULT

On the diagram below, sketch in and label a *stock*, *pedestal*, *slider*, and *trigger*.

Refer to *Catapult Design History* for help.

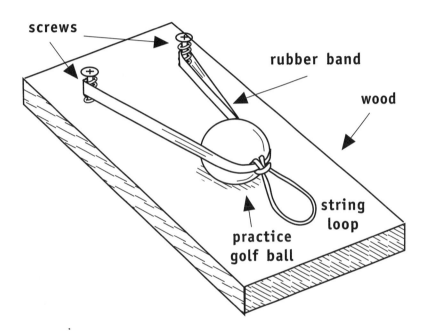

A Quick-Build Catapult

RESOURCE LIST—FASTENERS AND ADHESIVES

In the lists below, circle the fasteners and adhesives you will use in building your catapult and write which parts of the catapult will be joined with those fasteners next to your choice. For example:

(Binder clips) —— *to attach rubber band retainer to stock*

Be prepared to explain your choices in terms of cost, speed, durability, etc.

MECHANICAL FASTENERS	ADHESIVES
Screws	Transparent tape
Nails	Duct tape
Paper clips	Masking tape
Binder clips	Double-sided tape
Clamps	White glue (e.g., Elmer's™)
Rivets	Paste/glue sticks
Staples	Hot glue
Bolts and nuts	Construction adhesive
Hinges	Super glue
Wire	Velcro™ strips and dots
String	Adhesive foam mounting pads
Elastic bands	Contact cement
Clothespins	Rubber cement
Screw eyes	
Cup hooks	
Chain	
Pegs	
Slide/rail	
Clipboard	

NATIONAL SCIENCE TEACHERS ASSOCIATION

REDESIGN—A SECOND PASS

From your list in the previous activity, select the key variables you feel contributed most (positively or negatively) to the performance of your Quick-Build, and suggest what modifications you could make to meet the challenge goals. Record your current thinking below:

Most Significant Variables	Suggested Modifications

TEAM FEEDBACK FORM

Identify those variables that are interfering with the performance of the catapult. Make suggestions about what modifications could improve its performance.

Record the variables and suggested modifications in the table below:

Interfering Variables	Suggested Modifications

MAKING A FREQUENCY DISTRIBUTION

In the Challenge Event, you will exchange your catapult prototype and a User's Manual with those of another team who will be asked to hit a target by following your instructions—without the benefit of practice or trial and error. For your team to succeed in meeting the *Construct-a-Catapult* Design Challenge, you need to make a launching graph that will guide your partner team to successfully operate your catapult. The launching graph must relate the *force* used to pull back the slider to the *distance* the projectile goes. By referring to the User's Manual, the new team should be able to hit the target, no matter where it is placed.

Topic: presenting data
Go to: www.scilinks.org
Code: CAC07

You have probably seen variation in where the test projectiles land for a given force setting. You can refine your design and operating technique to reduce but not totally eliminate such variation. Statistical analysis of the variation will help you decide how to indicate and describe your catapult calibration markings for another user to interpret. The following activities will help you to find and describe patterns in your data variation. You can then use these patterns to make a launching graph that incorporates your calibration decisions.

First of all, you need to launch a number of projectiles at a variety of force settings and measure the distance they land from the catapult for each setting. Then make a series of frequency distributions so that you can analyze the spread pattern for your landing data.

Refer to your frequency distributions and describe the overall patterns of projectile landings. Note and discuss anything unusual you observe about your data. Your frequency distribution will go into your User's Manual.

MAKING A LAUNCHING GRAPH

Use the data from your frequency distributions to determine what distance, at each force setting, best represents the performance of your catapult for that force setting. Then, on a separate piece of paper, graph the relationship between amount of force (force setting) and distance traveled. Your launching graph will go into your User's Manual.

Once you have made your graph, answer the following questions:

1. Describe the general shape of your graph.

2. What do the data tell you about the relationship between the amount of force used to launch a projectile and the distance the projectile travels?

3. Hooke's Law states that stretch is proportional to the force applied. Does your graph indicate that distance traveled is also proportional to force applied?

What does your intuition, or knowledge of physics, suggest should be the relationship between force and distance traveled? [Hint: You may find the concept of energy conservation useful.]

REFLECTIONS ON YOUR DESIGN

1. What is the one feature of your catapult about which you are most proud?

2. Describe the concerns you have with the present design.

3. Describe in a paragraph or two the approach your team took in the designing and building of your catapult. Include a problem your team encountered with the performance of your catapult and how you went about solving it.

MATERIALS

FOR EACH STUDENT
Student Activity Sheets

- Beyond the Quick-Build (review)
- Parts of a Catapult
- Resource List—Fasteners and Adhesives
- Beyond the Quick-Build: Second Pass (assessment)
- Team Feedback Form
- Making a Frequency Distribution
- Making a Launching Graph
- Reflections on Your Design
- Design Process (optional)

FOR EACH TEAM
Calibration Materials

- roll of brown paper, 4–5 m in length
- safety glasses or goggles
- color-coding labels (assorted colors, round)
- graph paper
- meter sticks
- practice golf balls (or other lightweight projectiles)
- corn starch or chalk dust (for marking projectile landings)

FOR CLASS
Redesign Supplies

- screw eyes
- screw assortment
- rubber bands
- binder clips of different sizes
- bottle caps
- hinges
- corrugated board
- spring and straight clothespins
- lathe or wood molding strips

OVERVIEW—DEVELOPMENT

As homework, students may read the *Design Process* optional activity sheet (Appendix A, page 78) for use as a product development sequence. As part of their assignment, students could determine where in the activity loop they've been, where they are now, and where they'll go next.

On the Quick-Build Catapult diagram (page 41) students superimpose and label additional performance enhancement parts referred to in the *Catapult Design History* sheet. They will then compare their answers with those of their teammates to develop a common vocabulary for discussing diverse design elements.

Students review a list of alternative fasteners and adhesives, make choices, and construct a working model of their design. Students unfamiliar with fastening technology will benefit if choices are made by team consensus. Students do a second pass on identifying variables impeding performance—this time of their redesigned launcher—and record their suggested modifications.

Each team pairs with another team, trades catapults for evaluation, and makes and receives suggestions for modifications.

Students launch projectiles with their prototype in a testing arena; they record landings, describe patterns, and construct a frequency distribution. Students use their judgment to select representative data to: (1) graph for use as a launching guide; and (2) use as a basis for final calibrations and operational instructions for their prototype catapult.

Students reflect on their designs, describing both strengths and weaknesses.

Time Requirement

The overall time constraint of four days requires efficient and productive team pacing to accomplish the design, construction, and testing of catapult prototypes with one or more iteration. Encourage students throught this sequence to continue their team collaboration and to work intensively outside of class.

TEACHING SUGGESTIONS

Student teams will vary in how long they take to complete different stages of the prototype process. Therefore, the timing and the order of activities described below should be flexible.

Discussion of Homework: Design Process (optional)

Discuss the homework in *The Design Process* activity sheet. A good initial question to pose might be:

- Does the diagram depicting the design process accurately reflect your designing and building experience?

Other questions to ask from the homework:

- Which elements of this process have you already experienced?

- Where in the process do you think you are now?

You may wish to make the criteria you will use to assess students' technological design capability available at this point and invite discussion. Suggest to students that if they become stuck at any point they should refer again to their portfolio notebook for ideas about what to do next. Highlight, or elicit, examples of how students already used or might soon use the design process loop in non-linear progression.

Starting to Redesign the Catapult

Students may choose to proceed with the redesign of their catapults either by improving upon their Quick-Builds to make them more accurate, or by starting fresh. In either case, they should: (a) preserve or duplicate the elastic system they worked with in the research phase, or (b) re-calibrate a newly designed system. Advise them also to keep the users of their catapults in mind. Remind them that teams will be *exchanging* catapults to meet the final challenge. Therefore, students must make a catapult and instructions for operating it written in such a way that other students can operate the catapult easily and successfully.

Indicate the range of distances to target that may be employed in the final challenge, stressing that the exact distance will not be announced before the challenge. Operating instructions for the catapult must inform the user how to hit a target on the first attempt at any distance within the given range.

PREPARATION

- *Prepare fabrication zone: consider quantities of workspace, materials, tools, and fasteners available, and optimize spatial arrangements for safe, efficient access.*

- *Set up the launch testing arena: if space in your room allows, give each group its own area to launch its catapult. Alternatively, if there is not enough space for this, designate a "launching arena" for groups to share.*

- *For easy clean-up and convenient data recording, you may want students to prepare the launching arena. Roll out four to five meters of brown paper and tape it to the floor, making marks at meter intervals. Have colored sticky dots, cornstarch, or chalk dust available to mark the place where the projectile lands.*

- *Consider technological tools: if your students are proficient with computerized spreadsheet software or graphing calculators, the data they collect during test launches can be entered, manipulated, and printed. If they are not familiar with this technology, consider this an opportunity to demonstrate or expose them to the power of such tools.*

Resources for Redesigning

Before students begin redesigning, have them complete and discuss the *Parts of a Catapult* activity sheet—first individually, then as a team—to define the team's design vocabulary. They could also review the following resources to help them get started:

- *Beyond the Quick-Build*: a student activity sheet students did earlier (Activity 2, page 22), to refresh their memories about what kinds of modifications they need to make as they redesign their launchers;

- *Catapult Design History:* this includes diagrams and descriptions of types and parts of catapult stocks, pedestals, sliders, triggers, and propulsion systems;

- *Resource List—Fasteners and Adhesives*: a worksheet of possible ways to fasten parts of their prototype together.

Timely Feedback

As students move beyond their Quick-Builds, it is essential that teams be allowed to grapple with the challenges of designing, building, and testing their catapults—and of revisiting these processes. But it is also important that they receive input at critical times. One source of input is the team itself or perhaps a team launching nearby. Another important source is timely intervention from you. Very often, a suggestion about how to solve a problem, or a reference to a diagram or picture will stimulate action. Just be careful to avoid intervening too early and too often.

Evaluation and Reflection

After they have had a chance to struggle with the redesign of their catapults, or have become stuck, students have the opportunity to evaluate and reflect upon their redesign using the activity sheet, *Beyond the Quick-Build—Second Pass*.

You may wish to use the *Second Pass* activity sheet as a way of assessing students' growing ability to identify relevant variables. You might also assess their troubleshooting or problem-solving ability, as revealed in modifications they have made to address problems they have encountered.

Following this reflection/assessment, pair each team with another for the purpose of providing feedback about each other's catapults. Suggest to partner teams that they demonstrate their catapults to each other and that each team collaborate to provide written feedback to the other on the *Feedback* activity sheet. The goal here is two-fold: for students to share ideas and for them to obtain helpful feedback from others.

Both the *Second Pass* and the *Team Feedback Form* can be used more than once.

Once groups have consulted and provided feedback to each other, provide some time and space for each team to discuss and decide next steps.

Making a Force Scale

If students have not yet made markings for a force scale on their catapult, they have probably been using trial and error to hit their target. The force scale's purpose is to indicate as precisely as possible how far back the rubber band or slider should be pulled to apply specific force. Correlating landing distance with applied force is necessary for achieving repeatable results. Students should refer to the table they made in the research phase to relate stretch distance to force applied. They will most likely inscribe or attach the force scale on their sliders or stocks. To prevent a user from exceeding the limit of elasticity for their device (which would deform the elastic and render their markings useless), teams should consider making a slider stop or restraint.

Some catapult designs do not allow for a simple stretch scale along the slider. The trebuchet, for example, has no slider and is cocked with a rotating lever. Calibration can still be accomplished, however, using the same principles: use a calibrated rubber band to pull the rotating lever to a particular position. The stretch of the rubber band is still a measure of the force needed to reach that position.

Collecting Data

To test their catapults, students launch balls into the launching arena using a fixed launch angle and a range of force settings.

As each projectile is launched, it is helpful if one team member observes where it lands and puts a colored dot coded for the force setting at the landing place. Rolling the projectile into a powder such as colored chalk, cornstarch, or baking powder ahead of time makes the spot where it lands more visible.

Deciding How Good Is "Good Enough?"

Once groups start testing the accuracy of their catapults, it is important to discuss with them how accurate their catapults need to be. The answer to this question will depend upon your own goals and what is realistic, given the materials students are working with and their skills as problem solvers, designers, and builders. A suitable range of accuracy might be for the majority of balls launched at a given force setting to land at distances that are within 10–20% of each other. Alternatively, you might create a challenge event goal to land within a target zone (for example a pie tin) three out of five times.

Students will notice that even when they pull the slider back to the same place each time, the projectile does not always land in the same place; at best, the data will cluster within a certain range. Discuss with students ahead of time how many trials they think will give them a clear idea of the catapult's performance variation at that setting. This will depend on the accuracy that has been selected. In most cases, about 10 projectiles at each force setting should be adequate.

Whatever the standards you set for your students (or they set for themselves), remind them of the need to analyze and improve both the catapult system design and the operator launching techniques to achieve consistent performance. As your students are testing their catapults, look for evidence that they are evaluating and using their findings to make both system and operating improvement decisions.

Representing Data in a Frequency Distribution

To obtain a clear picture of their catapult's performance over a range of force settings and to show the spread of the data (variation or "error") at each of these force settings, students mark the landing points with dots or labels coded according to force setting, measure the distance each ball lands from the catapult, and represent these data graphically. As a visual record, they may wish to photograph the arena to show the overall landing patterns, draw an arena diagram, or, if paper was used on the arena floor, simply save the marked paper.

One way for them to represent patterns in their data quantitatively is with a frequency distribution. If your students have not had much experience describing data statistically, you may want to put a sample distribution on

Sample Frequency Distribution   Key: x = 1F, o = 2F, w = 3F, A = 4F the board and discuss as a class how to find which distance is most representative at a given force setting.

Students will display the patterns in their data on the *Making a Frequency Distribution* activity sheet.

Representing Data in a Line Graph

Students study the frequency distributions they made and determine a single distance that best represents the relationship of launch force to distance traveled for each data cluster. For a certain force setting, students may notice a mode or modal cluster in the data pattern and choose that distance as the most representative. In another situation, there may be no clear mode, and students may decide that the average best represents the performance of the catapult for that force setting. With such summary statistics of their data, students make a simple, clear launching graph for use in the Challenge Event, keeping in mind that others will have to understand it. Each team makes their custom launching graph on separate paper as part of the *Making a Launching Graph* activity sheet. This graph will be included later in their User's Manual. Addition of grid lines, error bars, and other enhancements should be reviewed by teams to describe whether

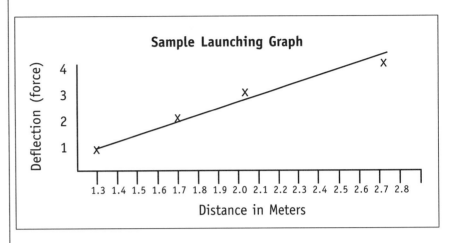

Sample Launching Graph

such enhancements would assist or confuse the prospective user in the Challenge Event.

Optional Extension: Projectile Motion

Students might compare their data to expectations from textbook descriptions and mathematical models of the parabolic paths of projectiles. They can determine the mass of the ball, apply known forces, observe, or even videotape trajectories and record landings. Most models apply to cases that have been simplified to ignore complicating effects of air friction. The projectiles used here, however, are acceptable in the classroom because they are specifically designed with low mass relative to surface area to capitalize on air friction and limit velocity and distance traveled. For these reasons, one cannot expect data from the catapults to follow frictionless models precisely.

By making comparisons of standard assumptions to real circumstances, students may better understand why different statistical summaries fit different force settings. This could lead them to create custom corrective factors for their launching graphs that are rooted in new conceptual understanding.

Design Self-Assessment

As a final development activity, students reflect upon what they have done thus far in *Reflections on Your Design*. They are asked to identify positives and negatives about their current design and to describe briefly their team approach and process. This activity sheet is short, and provides an opportunity for you to add questions of your own.

Assessing Students' Design and Build Capabilities

There are several key elements of students' design and build capabilities you could assess throughout the development phase:

- *How well students are able to develop solutions.* Developing ideas through to workable solutions is at the core of technological design. Look for evidence of students' ability to do this, both in your ongoing observations of students at work and in the responses they give on the activity sheet *Beyond the Quick-Build—Second Pass*.

- *How well students are able to evaluate the processes they have used.* This includes the extent to which they are able to identify strengths and weaknesses of their catapults. Look for evidence of students' ability to do this, both in your ongoing observations of students at work and in the responses they give on the activity sheet *Reflections on Your Design*.

- *To what extent do students exhibit ownership of the task?* Did it change with time? How much initiative did they take? Look for evidence of this in your ongoing observations of your students.

SAMPLE STUDENT CATAPULT DESIGNS

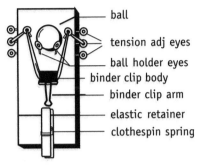

- ball
- tension adj eyes
- ball holder eyes
- binder clip body
- binder clip arm
- elastic retainer
- clothespin spring

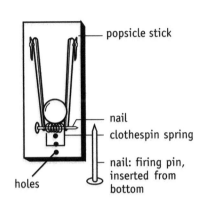

- popsicle stick
- nail
- clothespin spring
- nail: firing pin, inserted from bottom
- holes

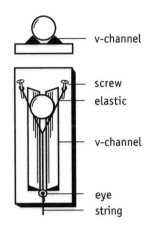

- v-channel
- screw
- elastic
- v-channel
- eye
- string

v-channel variations

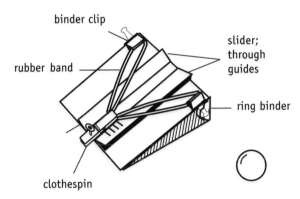

- binder clip
- slider; through guides
- rubber band
- ring binder
- clothespin

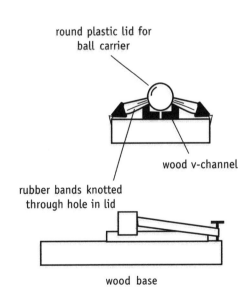

round plastic lid for ball carrier

wood v-channel

rubber bands knotted through hole in lid

wood base

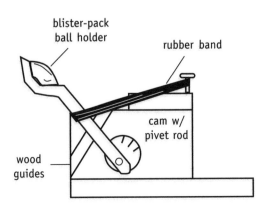

- blister-pack ball holder
- rubber band
- cam w/ pivet rod
- wood guides

Communication

OVERVIEW—COMMUNICATION

Your research and development team has made a prototype ready for demonstration in the final catapult Challenge Event. Now another team—using your draft written instructions—will operate your catapult in the event. For this reason, your team must communicate clear, effective operating instructions in a User's Manual that also summarizes and documents your efforts in constructing your catapult.

Think about the discoveries you have made while working through *Construct-a-Catapult*. Communicate the important science and technology topics that relate to your effort, and allow a prospective user to understand the principles involved.

Scope of Work

✿ Demonstrate the calibration accuracy of your prototype according to Challenge Event rules.

✿ As a team, write a User's Manual with instructions for others to successfully operate your catapult within performance specifications.

✿ Assess your own learning by comparing your post-project *Snapshot of Understanding* answers to those you wrote at the beginning of the unit.

✿ Submit your portfolio for individual assessment.

NATIONAL SCIENCE TEACHERS ASSOCIATION

CREATING A USER'S MANUAL

The final activity is for you to communicate the results of your work in a User's Manual. Your goal is to include information that would interest others in using your catapult and inform them about its capabilities.

An important skill for you to demonstrate in your User's Manual is the ability to communicate clearly about your catapult in writing. The writing of each section should be well organized and clear enough for someone unfamiliar with your team's catapult to understand.

You may find it interesting to consult several real user's manuals before you begin, but don't feel that yours needs to be just like these—any major appliance will have a user's manual, as will computer software or an electronic device. Have fun thinking about your own ways of describing your catapult.

Consult the Table of Contents shown below for a list of the topics you should address in your User's Manual. Some of these topics, like the launching graph or firing tips, have already been done. Others, like the mission statement or scientific principles of operation, still need to be written.

CATAPULT USER'S MANUAL
Table of Contents

I.   Team Mission Statement

II.   System Overview
       A.   Parts and Materials Specifications
       B.   Performance Specifications

III.   Operating Instructions
       A.   Safety Measures
       B.   Firing Tips
       C.   Launching Graph

IV.   The Science in Our Catapult

V. Appendices (Optional)
   A. Similar Product Comparisons
   B. Preventive Maintenance
   C. Repair and Re-calibration
   D. Disclaimers and Warranty

Members of your team should divide up the responsibility for writing each of the sections. Before you do so, read the suggestions below to obtain a clear idea of what each section is about.

Suggestions for User's Manual Sections

In your **Team Mission Statement,** state the purpose for your catapult. Take into consideration what your catapult's capabilities are as you think about what uses it could have. The mission statement should be a total team effort. First brainstorm as a team, then assign the actual writing to one member.

The **System Overview** includes a sketch of your catapult with labeled parts.

The **Parts and Materials Specifications** section lists details such as size, shape, composition, and quality of each component part.

The **Performance Specifications** section is the place to describe the capabilities of your product. What are the minimum and maximum distances your catapult can handle? How accurate is your catapult? (Your frequency distributions provide information about accuracy.)

The **Operating Instructions** should provide a step-by-step set of instructions for operating your catapult.

Safety Measures describe what precautions the user needs to take when using the catapult.

In the **Firing Tips** section, summarize your advice ("do's and don'ts") to the user. Provide as many tips as you can for helping the user get accurate and reliable performance.

For the **Launching Graph,** modify or explain how to use your existing launching guide in the context of your catapult's newly determined mission (purpose or intended use).

In the **Science in Our Catapult** section, discuss the scientific principles involved in the operation and use of your device. Consult and include the appropriate student activity sheets to address this topic.

Appendices are optional. Use them if you wish to include any of the following additional information:

- For *Product Comparisons*, describe each team's model in terms of its strengths and weaknesses. Think of yourself as a member of a large catapult manufacturer and your team's catapult as one in a range of choices for users with differing needs.

- For *Preventive Maintenance* advice, you might let the user know what kind of ongoing maintenance you think your catapult will need to continue performing well.

- *Repair* directions can address how to fix or rebuild the different parts when they break down.

- *Recalibration* directions could describe how to recalibrate your catapult's slider system if the elastic breaks or if the user wants to change the kind of elastic he or she is using.

- *Disclaimers and Warranty* address what parts your team as manufacturer will be responsible for should some repair be necessary and which parts you will not stand behind.

THE CHALLENGE EVENT

Usability Testing

To demonstrate you have met the *Construct-a-Catapult* Design Challenge you will put the prototype catapult you have designed and built to the ultimate test—having someone else operate it according to your instructions. This is comparable to "usability testing" in a real product development cycle. Similarly, you will be the user/tester of a partner team's unit.

Your teacher will provide details of the event structure and procedure. Ingredients for success may include:
- a clear and accurate User's Manual
- simple, understandable instruction (launching tips)
- durable construction
- well-tested, precise calibration clear to any user

Notes

Use the space below to record your teacher's detailed instructions and criteria for success for the challenge event, as well as your own thoughts and reminders both before and after the event.

NATIONAL SCIENCE TEACHERS ASSOCIATION

S N A P S H O T
of Understanding: **W**hat I *Now* Know About Catapults

1. (a) What variables are important to control for catapult accuracy?

   (b) What scientific principle(s) can you use to describe how the catapult you designed and built operates?

2. What are the main features of a catapult? Make a sketch and label its parts, or describe.

3. List current uses of catapult-like devices of which you are aware.

4. Describe how you went about designing and building your catapult.

5. What do the following terms mean?

force:

energy:

3 DAYS

OVERVIEW—COMMUNICATION

Teams summarize what they have learned about their catapult by creating a User's Manual that includes information about how to use their catapult, how it is constructed, its principles of operation, and performance specifications. A sample of topics for students to address, along with explanatory text, is provided on the *Creating a User's Manual* activity sheet. In the Challenge Event, teams exchange catapults and launching graphs, with associated instructions and firing tips. Each team operates another team's prototype. The most succesful design is the one that could be used most accurately by another team.

As a final assessment, students answer questions similar to those at the very beginning of the unit in the final *Snapshot of Understanding*.

Time Requirement

This unit can be conducted in three class sessions:

- One class for writing team User's Manual (plus homework)
- One class for the Challenge Event
- One class for reflection and final self-assessment

TEACHING SUGGESTIONS

Creating the User's Manual

Discuss with your students which topics to include in their User's Manuals and suggest that they develop a plan for delegating parts of the writing within their teams. Also suggest that they take into consideration what the strengths and weaknesses of their catapult may be compared to the catapults of other teams. This may help them consider how to write instructions that can be used by students who are used to another kind of catapult.

Encourage teams to test drafts of their User's Manual with people from the other teams rather than with members of their own team. At the same time, within each team, every person should review the other members' sections before the report is assembled.

If time permits, include a brainstorming session for possible uses or markets for the catapults. Examples could be delivering waste paper to the circular file, passing cherry tomatoes at the dinner table, or providing an automatic partner for ping pong practice.

MATERIALS

FOR EACH STUDENT
Student Activity Sheets
- The Challenge Event— Usability Testing
- Creating a User's Manual
- Snapshot of Understanding

FOR EACH TEAM
- *safety glasses or goggles*
- *target for the Challenge Event*
- *word processing or graphics stations as available (optional)*

PREPARATION

- *Prepare a Challenge Event plan, location, and procedure.*
- *Consider offering spectator invitations, competitive aspect, and focus on launching guides.*
- *Provide (or have students bring in) a few different examples of user's manuals.*
- *Customize the User's Manual Table of Contents to fit the time and educational objectives for your class (or encourage students to make such decisions).*
- *Prepare a grading plan for your evaluation of the team and individual effort.*
- *Arrange for use of word processing/graphics (or CAD) computer stations (optional).*
- *Arrange flexible seating to facilitate team discussions and writing (optional).*

During the Challenge Event, the ability to communicate clearly in writing via a User's Manual may prove to be more important than the design and construction of the catapult. Remind students that whether in science or technology, clear communication of purpose, method, and process is not only required, it is often the most important element of success in the marketplace.

Meeting the Construct-a-Catapult Challenge

Remind all students to wear safety glass or goggles, particularly in the launching or landing zones.

When groups have completed their User's Manuals, it is time to conduct the Challenge Event. Arrange a system for groups to exchange catapults. To avoid advance coaching, do not tell teams ahead of time which team gets which catapult. The target range you select should also be unpredictable.

To choose a target distance, you may wish to examine students' data to find a target distance that lies between data points already measured. Alternatively, you might select outside their data range, requiring students to interpolate or extrapolate.

Make sure that accurate data is maintained on every team's operation of the catapult so that fair comparisons can be made and the performance of each catapult can be ranked.

If time permits after the Challenge Event, consider the following questions in a class discussion:

- Which catapult had the greatest variation in data? Which characteristics of this catapult could account for this variation?

- Which catapult demonstrated the greatest accuracy? Which characteristics of this catapult could account for its accuracy?

- Did each team operate the catapult according to instructions? If not, were the user operating procedures at fault, or did the team misread them?

Continue the discussion in the following class period, leaving just enough time for students to complete the second *Snapshot*.

Completing the Snapshot of Understanding

After students complete the final *Snapshot of Understanding* (allow about 20 minutes), provide a brief time for them to compare their new answers with those on their pre-unit Snapshot. (Hand the first *Snapshot* back at this time.) It can be very empowering for students to see for themselves how much they have learned.

NATIONAL SCIENCE TEACHERS ASSOCIATION

Side Roads

SIDE ROADS

The following pages correspond to the Side Road suggestions made in each activity. Many of these are key activities, but they have been placed in the Side Roads section because they can fit in several different places—exactly where they are used is a matter best decided by you in response to student questions and feedback.

Some activities may be profitably used more than once. An analysis of the design process, for example, will provide different insights in the Research activity section than those of the Design activities.

In this section:

- 📂 Internet Information Search
- 📂 Homework—Individual Information Search
- 📂 Inquiry Process
- 📂 Projectile Motion
- 📂 Design Process
- 📂 Additional Suggestions

INTERNET INFORMATION SEARCH

If at all possible, prepare for a quick demonstration showing students the steps and what to expect—either real-time or pre-taped via feed to large screen TV monitor in the classroom.

A few cautionary words about censorship, commercialism, and privacy issues should be included at the outset. Consult your school policy and lab director for assistance.

Set an objective, assignment, or contest that requires each student or pair of students to turn in a search path or research result printout at the end of the session. Inform students how the deliverable will be used for assessment.

Schedule enough time for the activity so that slow navigators will reach satisfying pre-determined destinations (with provisions for speedsters to move beyond).

Consider pairing students: inexperienced with familiar, confident with scared, leaders with followers, disciplinary problems with angels, etc., to create peer teaching opportunities and reduce individual distractions from allowing you to gain group attention.

Pairing will also decrease the network traffic in your lab that could otherwise decrease computer response times.

If your lab or media center administrator has not already done so, prepare a brief but precise list of sequential steps to start up, log on, connect to the Internet, and select and arrive at a search screen. Duplicate and provide as a handout to each pair of navigators. Some "Don'ts" may need to be listed, such as do not double click, with easy-to-remember explanations like machines hate to be told twice or more technical reasons such as slowing the processor to sort through duplicate instructions and exceeding memory to open and display duplicate screens.

The structure of search commands will have to be covered, as well as how to limit a search by combining key words. You might want to prepare a list of key words you have tried and found productive for groups to pick from according to their interests or assigned objective. Having everyone achieve a common destination and then diverge will increase the class's overall depth of exploration if results are to be shared.

You may wish to show students how to create bookmarks and then print their list of bookmark addresses so they can return to interesting sites later, outside of class. After the search, you may wish to provide a list of known web sites from your own reference and resource list and invite students to submit additions to it. Providing short-cut instructions on how to GO TO or OPEN a known URL as distinct from the search procedures just conducted will be helpful to avoid confusion.

The following URLs were active and helpful during the development of the curriculum:

- The Grey Company Trebuchet Page: http://www.iinet.net.au/ ~rmine/gctrebs.html

- There is an on-line "Catapult Museum" site: http:// www.nzp.com/index.html

- Related to catapults is archery: http://ericir.syr.edu/Projects/ Newton/10/lessons/Archery.html

HOMEWORK—INDIVIDUAL INFORMATION SEARCH

The introduction to this unit on catapults gives you a sense of the variety of forms and uses of the machine. The pictures included show three different types of catapult: the onager, the ballista, and the trebuchet. Select one of the three types of catapults and perform an in-depth information search. Use the questions outlined below as a guide, and put together a report for the class that includes illustrations, written materials, and a list of relevant references for those who wish to explore your topic further.

I. The history of your type of catapult:
   A. For what purpose was this type of catapult used or designed?
   B. Did it persist in use for the original purpose?
   C. How did its uses and/or purposes change through history?
   D. Are there contemporary uses of the device itself, or as part of another machine? Give examples.

II. The design of your type of catapult:
   A. Describe the original design. Use illustrations to identify parts and their functions, and materials used.
   B. Was the original design modified throughout history? How and why?
   C. Has the original catapult of this type been supplanted by some other machine? What and why?
   D. Are there other machines that incorporate this device? Give examples.

III. The science and technology in your catapult:
   A. What scientific principles or disciplines contributed to the design?
   B. What technologies were applied to create this type of catapult?

IV. References you used and recommend:
   A. Books
   B. Articles
   C. Films, videos
   D. Web sites

INQUIRY PROCESS

The *inquiry process* is often viewed as a cycle of action that repeats until the investigators reach a satisfying solution. It can be described with seven basic elements:

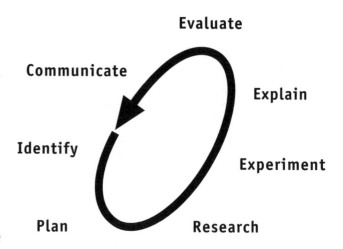

Identify and clarify questions. Understand the issue or problem, and make a testable hypothesis.

Plan appropriate procedures. Brainstorm, draw and write ideas, clarify ideas, and suggest possible strategies or methods.

Research major concepts. Learn what is known about the situation from sources other than actual investigation, and obtain information from preliminary experiments. Decide what technology, approach, equipment, and safety precautions are useful. Document your experiments and log your data.

Experiment. Use tools and measuring devices to conduct experiments. Use calculators and computers to store and present data.

Explain logical connections. Analyze your data. Formulate explanations using logic and evidence, and possibly by constructing a physical, conceptual, or mathematical model.

Evaluate alternatives. Compare your explanations to current scientific understanding and other plausible models. Identify what needs to be revised, and find the preferred solution.

Communicate new knowledge and methods. Communicate results of your inquiry to your peers and others in the community. Construct a reasoned argument through writing, drawings, and oral presentations. Respond appropriately to critical comments.

NATIONAL SCIENCE TEACHERS ASSOCIATION

Questions

Read the following questions, but do not answer them until after your team has experienced working together on the design challenge research activities.

Topic: scientific inquiry
Go to: www.scilinks.org
Code: CAC08

1. Make your own checklist of team activities that correspond to steps in the cycle described above:

2. Create your own version of the inquiry process using words and pathways that fit your team's activity.

3. What shape is your inquiry pathway diagram (circle, spiral, cascade, other)?

4. How and where do the seven steps described on page 69 fit within your process description?

PROJECTILE MOTION

A projectile is any object that has been launched into the air and moves freely under only the influences of gravity and air resistance. The effect of gravity is a constant downward acceleration from the moment of launching, usually specified with the value: g = 9.81m/s2. The effect of air resistance is often relatively small and/or difficult to predict as a combination of object surface drag, air speed, and direction.

Launch Angle Effect

The angle of launch is significant because angles above the horizontal add an upward component of velocity against the acceleration of gravity, increasing the time of flight (but not necessarily the horizontal distance traveled) before landing. A typical two-dimensional graph of projectile motion (here using $\emptyset = 45°$ and $v_o = 5$ m/sec) is a parabola:

$$y = x \tan 45 - \frac{9.81}{2 \times 5^2 \cos^2 45} x^2$$

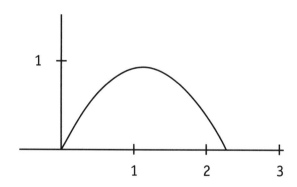

On the graph above, superimpose sketches of the trajectory curves you would expect for similar projectiles launched with equal force, but at angles of 60° and 30°. At what launch angle(s) do you expect to obtain: (a) greatest horizontal distance? (b) greatest vertical height?

HISTORICAL NOTE

The ENIAC computer was created in 1946, using 18,000 vacuum tubes, at a cost of $500,000 to calculate ballistic trajectories.

NATIONAL SCIENCE TEACHERS ASSOCIATION

Air Resistance Effect

When precise prediction is not required, air resistance is often not calculated. In the Construct-a-Catapult Design Challenge, air resistance is an important factor in the behavior of practice golf balls used as projectiles. A key design criterion for practice golf balls is to limit the distance of travel without skewing direction. This performance characteristic is useful for the scale of construction and testing possible within the classroom.

Research air resistance effects on projectiles and list the factors you discover in the space below. Seek formulae for mathematical expression of air resistance and describe how to experimentally quantify a "damping coefficient" for your projectile.

Initial Velocity Effect

Refer to your launching graph and use your prior knowledge about Newton's Second Law of Motion (F=ma) and your findings about air resistance to explain any changes observed in the relationship between applied force and distance at increasing velocities.

Topic: force
Go to: www.scilinks.org
Code: CAC01

Topic: energy
Go to: www.scilinks.org
Code: CAC02

Topic: elasticity
Go to: www.scilinks.org
Code: CAC03

Topic: gravity
Go to: www.scilinks.org
Code: CAC05

Topic: friction
Go to: www.scilinks.org
Code: CAC09

DESIGN PROCESS

The *design process* is often viewed as a cycle of action that repeats until the designers reach a satisying solution. It can be described with seven basic elements:

Identify and clarify the situation. Understand the challenge or problem, including the criteria for success and constraints on the design.

Create solutions. Brainstorm, draw and write ideas, and suggest possible strategies or methods.

Investigate possibilities. Learn what is known about the situation and what technology or approach could be useful. Conduct experiments to test your ideas.

Choose a solution. List the solutions most likely to be successful, and make decisions for how well each solution meets the design challenge or solves the problem.

Implement the design. Learn that a successful design often depends on good fabrication, whether it is a scaled or life-sized version of the product.

Evaluate the design. Perform tests to obtain the feedback that informs them about the parts of the design that worked or needed improvement.

Communicate the solution. Present your designs to your peers and others in the community, communicating your ideas through drawings, writing, formal presentations, or informal discussions.

NATIONAL SCIENCE TEACHERS ASSOCIATION

Questions

After reading about the design process, answer the following questions:

1. What elements of the process have you already experienced?

2. What elements have you not yet experienced?

3. Where in the process do you think you are now?

4. What will your next steps be?

ADDITIONAL SUGGESTIONS

If you are comfortable with calculus, you may want to point out that energy is calculated by the area under a force vs. stretch graph. In the case of Hooke's Law, the graph will be a straight line of slope k. The area under the graph will be a triangle and the equation $E = (1/2)kS^2$ is the area of a triangle of base S and height kS.

You should be well prepared for the likelihood that students will have lots of questions such as "What triangle produces $(1/2)mv^2$?"

NATIONAL SCIENCE TEACHERS ASSOCIATION

Text Reconstruction Exercises

TEXT RECONSTRUCTION

The jumbled paragraphs in the following reading assignments are examples of Text Reconstruction (TR). This well-established technique for reading and writing improvement has roots going back to Benjamin Franklin as well as a number of famous authors. Many teachers find that including TR in a reading assignment highly motivates students and results in a much higher rate of homework completion. We suggest you read Chapter 5 of *Why Johnny Can't Write* for complete instructions on how to design your own exercises. Additional exercises can be found in *How to Analyze, Organize, & Write Effectively*.

An instructional process that uses design or inquiry places great demands on class time. It is impossible to cover all essential content within the few hours per week students spend in class. Science and technology courses must therefore insist that students learn from reading. This means they must also provide realistic opportunities for students to improve their ability to learn from reading.

Text Reconstruction works as a method of improving reading skills by focusing student attention on the most important elements of the reading task. First, it changes the reader's perception of his or her role from that of a passive absorber of information to that of an active agent who must sort out a puzzle. This is probably the main reason TR exercises are popular with students. Secondly, TR forces students to pay attention to the logic of a paragraph. In science, it is not the separate ideas that are important, but rather the logic that ties them together. When passively reading a paragraph, one can easily miss that logic, but in TR it is impossible to complete the task without thoroughly understanding these interconnections. A student who reconstructs a paragraph will understand its structure and meaning far more deeply than a student who memorizes every word but considers them only in their current order.

In the *Science by Design* series, we employ various techniques to encourage student reading and writing. These are not extras but rather essential elements of the program. The exercises included assume that your students are relatively strong readers. If your students are weak readers or are not used to serious homework, then you will need to increase the amount of attention you pay to improving reading skills. Text Reconstruction can be used to convert any kind of reading assignment into a stimulating puzzle. The more use you make of TR, the more your students will read and the better they will understand.

For more information on Text Reconstruction Across the Curriculum contact: The Institute for TRAC Research, P.O. Box 7336, Albuquerque NM. Tel. (505) 831-2654 or visit the New Intelligence *Web site at* http://www.newintel.com

KEY IDEAS EXPLAINED

Each key idea Text Reconstruction sheet covers one key science idea that is used in *Construct-a-Catapult*. The first execise sheet, Force, involves a very simple reconstruction and is intended as an introduction to TR. The later sheets involve much more difficult reconstructions.

FORCE TEXT RECONSTRUCTION EXERCISE

The paragraphs below describe how the concept of force can help you better understand the workings of your catapult. To prevent this information from falling into the wrong hands, the order of the sentences in each paragraph has been jumbled. Your task is to rearrange the sentences in their correct order. Good luck.

Force

¶1 _____ The reason it is difficult is that it is similar but not entirely the same as the concept we use in everyday speech.

_____ The concept of force as it is used in physics is both simple and, at the same time, very difficult to understand.

_____ The best advice we can give is to look for these differences.

_____ Gradually you will gain enough experience to understand the physics way of talking.

¶2 _____ His second law: $F = ma$, states that forces affect not the speed of an object but rather the rate of change of speed.

_____ Isaac Newton became famous by discovering how force was related to motion.

_____ A constant force will make an object go faster and faster and faster...

¶3 _____ There are two kinds of force you need to know how to calculate for designing a catapult.

_____ The second force is gravity.

_____ It is given by the equation $F = mg$, where g is the acceleration of gravity (on the surface of the earth that is 9.8 meters/(second)2) and m is the mass being pulled by gravity.

_____ The force of pull of a stretched rubber band is given by Hooke's Law: $F = kS$, where S is the amount of stretch of the rubber band.

NATIONAL SCIENCE TEACHERS ASSOCIATION

ELASTICITY TEXT RECONSTRUCTION EXERCISE

The paragraphs below describe how the concept of elasticity can help you better understand the workings of your catapult. To prevent this information from falling into the wrong hands, the order of the sentences in each paragraph has been jumbled. Your task is to rearrange the sentences in their correct order. Good luck.

Elasticity

_____ There are deformations beyond which there is no return.

¶1

_____ A rubber ball is usually a good example of a highly elastic object; a window pane is a good example of a less elastic object.

_____ Everything is elastic to some extent but every object also has limits.

_____ The elastic property of matter is its ability to deform under forces and to return to its original shape when the forces are removed.

¶2

_____ You push twice as hard and you will get twice the deformation.

_____ In this case, the idea that Force (F) is proportional to Stretch (S) can be expressed as $F = kS$.

_____ This is most easily seen in a rubber band which will stretch some amount for one unit of force and twice as far for two units of force.

_____ Hooke's Law states that the region of elasticity is governed by a rule in which the amount of deformation is proportional to the applied force.

_____ When two variables are directly proportional, they always follow one very simple mathematical equation of the form $A = kB$.

ENERGY TEXT RECONSTRUCTION EXERCISE

The paragraphs below describe how the concept of energy can help you better understand the workings of your catapult. To prevent this information from falling into the wrong hands, the order of the sentences in each paragraph has been jumbled. Your task is to rearrange the sentences in their correct order. Good luck.

Energy

¶1

_____ As long as the catapult is cocked, this energy remains hidden in the elastic (physicists call this hidden energy "potential").

_____ In this equation, E stands for energy, k the elastic constant (different for each rubber band), and S is the amount of stretch.

_____ The energy stored in an elastic medium (a rubber band in our case) can be calculated from the formula $E = (1/2)kS^2$.

_____ When you fire a spring-loaded catapult, you convert elastic potential energy to kinetic energy.

¶2

_____ If we assume all the energy goes into the projectile, we can equate the two energy equations and write: $(1/2)mv^2 = (1/2)kS^2$.

_____ In this equation, E stands for energy, m for mass, and v for velocity.

_____ After the catapult fires, the energy appears in the projectile as "kinetic" energy.

_____ Some energy disappears in friction and recoil but we usually ignore these factors.

_____ The kinetic energy of any moving object can be calculated from the equation $E = (1/2)mv^2$.

_____ The catapult in which friction and recoil can realistically be ignored is called an "ideal" catapult.

FORCE TEXT RECONSTRUCTION KEY

The three paragraphs below show the correct order of sentences in the Force Text Reconstruction exercise.

Paragraph 1

1. The concept of force as it is used in physics is both simple and, at the same time, very difficult to understand.

2. The reason it is difficult is that it is similar but not entirely the same as the concept we use in everyday speech.

3. The best advice we can give is to look for these differences.

4. Gradually you will gain enough experience to understand the physics way of talking.

Paragraph 2

1. Isaac Newton became famous by discovering how force was related to motion.

2. His second law: $F = ma$, states that forces affect not the speed of an object but rather the rate of change of speed.

3. A constant force will make an object go faster and faster and faster...

Paragraph 3

1. There are two kinds of force you need to know how to calculate for designing a catapult.

2. The force of pull of a stretched rubber band is given by Hooke's Law: $F = kS$, where S is the amount of stretch of the rubber band.

3. The second force is gravity.

4. It is given by the equation $F = mg$, where g is the acceleration of gravity (on the surface of the earth that is 9.8 meters/(second)2.) and m is the mass being pulled by gravity.

Topic: energy
Go to: www.scilinks.org
Code: CAC02

Topic: elasticity
Go to: www.scilinks.org
Code: CAC03

Topic: gravity
Go to: www.scilinks.org
Code: CAC05

Topic: mass
Go to: www.scilinks.org
Code: CAC06

Topic: friction
Go to: www.scilinks.org
Code: CAC09

ELASTICITY TEXT RECONSTRUCTION KEY

The two paragraphs below show one correct way to order the sentences in the Elasticity Text Reconstruction exercise. There may be other reasonable orders but you should accept them only if students can justify their choices.

Paragraph 1

1. The elastic property of matter is its ability to deform under forces and to return to its original shape when the forces are removed.

2. Everything is elastic to some extent but every object also has limits.

3. There are deformations beyond which there is no return.

4. A rubber ball is usually a good example of a highly elastic object; a window pane is a good example of a less elastic object.

Paragraph 2

1. Hooke's Law states that the region of elasticity is governed by a rule in which the amount of deformation is proportional to the applied force.

2. You push twice as hard and you will get twice the deformation.

3. This is most easily seen in a rubber band that will stretch some amount for one unit of force and twice as far for two units of force.

4. When two variables are directly proportional, they always follow one very simple mathematical equation of the form $A = kB$.

5. In this case, the idea that Force (F) is proportional to Stretch (S) can be expressed as $F = kS$.

NATIONAL SCIENCE TEACHERS ASSOCIATION

ENERGY TEXT RECONSTRUCTION KEY

The two paragraphs below show one correct way to order the sentences in the Energy Text Reconstruction exercise. There may be other reasonable orders but you should accept them only if students can justify their choices.

Paragraph 1

1. When you fire a spring-loaded catapult, you convert elastic potential energy to kinetic energy.

2. The energy stored in an elastic medium (a rubber band in our case) can be calculated from the formula $E = (1/2)kS2$.

3. In this equation, E stands for energy, k the elastic constant (different for each rubber band), and S is the amount of stretch.

4. As long as the catapult is cocked, this energy remains hidden in the elastic (physicists call this hidden energy "potential.")

Paragraph 2

1. After the catapult fires, the energy appears in the projectile as "kinetic" energy.

2. Some energy disappears in friction and recoil but we usually ignore these factors.

3. The catapult in which friction and recoil can realistically be ignored is called an "ideal" catapult.

4. The kinetic energy of any moving object can be calculated from the equation $E = (1/2)mv2$.

5. In this equation, E stands for energy, m for mass, and v for velocity.

6. If we assume all the energy goes into the projectile, we can equate the two energy equations and write: $(1/2)mv2 = (1/2)kS2$.

Sample Answers

IDENTIFYING VARIABLES

Activity 2, p. 21

Parts of the Catapult System	
VARIABLE	**RANGE OF VARIATION**
Example: *Angle of the catapult*	*flat, between 0° and 45°, between 45° and 90°*
Stretch of elastic	A little—really breaks
Constrain projectile to center of run	No adjustment available
User Operating Procedures	
VARIABLE	**RANGE OF VARIATION**
Example: *How you position the rubber band*	*high on the nails, in the middle of the nails, low on the nails*
How you let go	Slowly—quickly
Even out pull of left and right elastic	No alignment—careful alignment

BEYOND THE QUICK-BUILD

Activity 2, p. 22

Most Significant Variables	Suggested Modifications
amount of pull on elastic	need repeatable scale
even lift and right pull of elastic	design for automatic connection
angle of launch	variable and accurate settings
release of projectile	design trigger release

Activity 3, p. 29 **INVESTIGATING ELASTICITY**

Experimenting with Stretch

Elastic A: *about 3 in. long; wide, stiff, short stretch*

Elastic B: *about 4 in. long; narrow, long stretch*

Activity 3, pp. 31–33 ## Questions 5–10

5. (a) Describe what you noticed about the points plotted for each rubber band.
       Same amount of stretch for each weight added

    (b) Could a straight line include all or most of your data for each rubber band? Explain.
       Straight line fits most data, but not data near the end

6. Use your graph to predict the distance of stretch for masses smaller and larger than those you used.
    (a) How accurate do you think these predictions will be? Explain.
       In the middle of the range, the data will be accurate; at the end, not so good.

    (b) Pick a mass between that of two you used. For example, if you had used 45 grams and 60 grams in your calibration, choose a mass in between—perhaps 55 grams. Figure out the length of the stretch corresponding to this applied mass.
       Band A: .2 kg is .4"   .3 kg is .6"   .25 kg will be .5"

    c. What do you think happens in the case of very large applied masses? Explain.
       Band breaks. Band is only so strong.

7. Try to express the relationship between mass and distance as a formula.
    For Band A, Stretch = 2x weight

8. Hooke's Law states that the stretch is proportional to the mass you applied. The region in which a material—in this case the rubber band—obeys Hooke's Law is called the *elastic limit* of the material.
    (a) What does your graph tell you about the elasticity of your rubber bands?
       Limit is near .5 kg; after that, stretch 2 x wt.

9. (a) Plot both lines from the graphs you made in question 4 on the same set of coordinates.

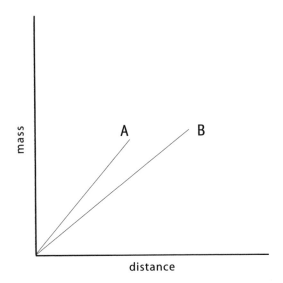

(b) Compare the two lines and explain similarities and differences between them. Be sure to compare them with regard to their conformity to expectations from Hooke's Law.

B stretches more than A

(c) What do you think the area under your plotted lines represents?
Something to do with how hard you pull. [Note: units are weight times distance. Force X distance = work; hence, units are units of energy.]

10. How could this exercise help you design your mechanical launching system?
Can build scale to show how hard you have pulled on the rubber band.

Activity 4, p. 43 **REDESIGN—A SECOND PASS**

Most Significant Variables	Suggested Modifications
lack of even left-right pull	center projectile on rubber band
projectile veers left or right	make groove on track
angle shifts at firing	build solid system for launch angle control

Activity 4, p. 44 **TEAM FEEDBACK FORM**

Interfering Variables	Suggested Modifications
slider is sloppy	redesign
pedestal not rigid	redesign
screws bend	tighten or design better attachment for rubber band

NATIONAL SCIENCE TEACHERS ASSOCIATION

ballista: a stone-thrower catapult usually using a crossbow design

best-fit line: a smooth line drawn through the scatter of data points plotted on a graph leaving as many points below the line as above

brainstorm: a group problem-solving technique which involves the spontaneous contribution of ideas from all members of the group

calibrate, calibration: determining a measurement scale or aligning a device with a measurement scale

catapult: a device used to throw things

dynamics: a branch of physics related to the effect of forces

elastic limit: the maximum stretch that can be applied before the stretch no longer obeys Hooke's Law (usually damage is done to the elastic when it is stretched beyond this limit).

elasticity: the property that allows an object to stretch and return to its original length

energy transfer: the movement of energy from one place to another or from one form to another

forces: pushes and pulls

frequency distribution: a tabulation of the number of times events happen

iterative processes: processes that are repeated over and over; usually gradually approaching some goal

kinematics: a branch of physics related to motion

milestones: key markers along some process that provide a rough measure of progress toward some goal

onager: a type of catapult similar in design to that of the common mouse-trap, in which a projectile is held in a rope sling to give it extra thrust

optimize: to design for best results

optimization: the process of discovering optimal conditions

pawl: a toothed wheel used in a ratchet

portfolio: a collection of products or designs

prototype: an original model; first full-scale and (usually) functional form of a new type of construction

ratchet: a device that allows an axle to rotate in one direction but not another; usually involves a saw-toothed wheel and a spring lever that catches the teeth so as to prevent backward rotation

siege: a tactic used in warfare where the enemy is surrounded and cut-off from sources of supply and support

sinew: fibrous material that can be twisted or stretched

spring constant: the constant in Hooke's Law that relates the amount of stretch to the amount of force

tension: a force pulling or stetching a body

torsion: a force twisting a body

trebuchet, trebouchet: a catapult that works like an unbalanced seesaw

variable: an object or quality of changeable value

References

American Association for the Advancement of Science. 1993. *Project 2061: Benchmarks for Science Literacy*. New York: Oxford University Press.

Bennett, K. E., and W.C. Ward. 1993. *Construction versus Choice in Cognitive Measurement: Issues in Constructed Response, Performance Testing, and Portfolio Assessment*. Hillsdale, NJ: L. Erlbaum Associates.

Chevedden, P. E., Eigenbrod, L., Foley, V., and W. Soedel. 1995. The trebuchet. *Scientific American*, July:66-71.

Corfis, I. and M. Wolfe. 1995. Artillery in late antiquity: Prelude to the Middle Ages. In P. E. Chevedden, *The Medieval City Under Siege*. Suffolk, U.K.: Boydell & Brewer Press.

Gartrell, J.E. 1990. *Methods of Motion: An Introduction to Mechanics*. Washington, DC: National Science Teachers Association.

Germann, P. J., Haskins, S., and S. Auls. 1996. Analysis of nine high school biology laboratory manuals: Promoting scientific inquiry. *Journal of Research in Science Teaching* 33(5):475–499.

Gitomer, D.H. 1988. Individual differences in technical troubleshooting. *Human Performance* 1(2):111-131.

Gokhale, A. 1997. Writing in the technology discipline. *The Technology Teacher* 56(8):11–23.

Haas, N. and C. Boston. 1994. One school experiments with performance-based assessments. *The Eric Review*. 3:13–14.

International Technology Education Association. 1996. *Technology for All Americans: A Rationale and Structure for the Study of Technology*.

Keys, C. W. 1995. An interpretive study of students' use of scientific reasoning during a collaborative report writing intervention in ninth grade general science. *Science Education* 79(4):415–435.

——. 1994. The development of scientific reasoning skills in conjunction with collaborative writing assignments: An interpretive study of six ninth grade students. *Journal of Reesarch in Science Teaching* 31(9):1003–1022.

Linden, M.J. 1990. *Why Johnny Can't Write: How to Improve Writing Skills*. Hillsdale, NJ: L. Erlbaum.

National Council for Teachers of Mathematics. 1991. *Professional Standards for Teaching Mathematics*. Reston, VA: NCTM.

National Research Council. 1996. *National Science Education Standards*. Washington DC: National Academy Press.

Naveh-Benjamine, M., and Y. Lin. 1991. *Assessing student's origination of concepts: A manual for measuring course-specific knowledge structures*. Ann Arbor: National Center for Research to Improve Postsecondary Teaching and Learning, University of Michigan.

Payne-Gallwey, R. 1995. *The Book of the Crossbow*. NY: Dover Publications.

Petroski, H. 1996. *Invention by Design: How Engineers Get from Thought to Thing*. Cambridge, MA: Harvard University Press.

Raizen, S. A., Sellwood, P., Todd, R. D., and M. Vickers. 1995. *Technology Education in the Classroom: Understanding the Designed World*. San Francisco: The National Center for Improving Science Education, Jossey-Bass Publisher.

Richmond, G. and J. Striley. 1996. Making meaning in classroom: Social processes in small-group discourse and scientific knowledge building. *Journal of Research in Science Teaching* 33(8):839–858.

Roth, W. M., and G. M. Bowen. 1995. Knowing and interacting: A study of culture, practices and resources in a grade 8 open-inquiry science classroom guided by a cognitive apprenticeship metaphor. *Cognition And Instruction* 13(1):73–128.

Rudner, L., and C. Boston. 1994. Performance assessment. *The Eric Review* 3:2–12.

Soedel, W. and V. Foley. 1979. Ancient catapults. *Scientific American*, March:150–174.

Task Force on Social Studies Teacher Education Standards. 1997. *National Standards for Social Studies Teachers*. Washington, DC: National Council for the Social Studies.

Warry, J. 1995. *Warfare in the Classical World*. Norman, OK: University of Oklahoma Press

Whimby, A. 1987. *Analyze, Organize, Write: A Structured Program for Expository Writing*. Hillsdale, NJ: L. Erlbaum.

Wong, E.D. 1993. Understanding the generative capacity of analogies as a tool for explanation. *Journal of Research in Science Teaching* 30(10):1259-1272.